Holly Roberts

Holly Roberts

Introduction by David Featherstone

Untitled 50
The Friends of Photography
San Francisco

This publication has been made possible through
the generous support of Valerie K. Maslak.

Untitled 50
*This is the fiftieth in a series of publications
on serious photography by The Friends of Photography.
Some previous issues are still available.
For a list of these, write to Publication Sales, The Friends
of Photography, Ansel Adams Center,
250 Fourth Street, San Francisco, California 94103.*

The Friends of Photography
*The Friends of Photography, founded in 1967
in Carmel, California, is a not-for-profit membership
organization housed in the Ansel Adams Center
in San Francisco. The programs of The Friends in publications,
exhibitions, education and awards to photographers
are guided by a commitment to photography
as a fine art and to the discussion of photographic ideas
through critical inquiry. The publications of
The Friends, along with admission to the Ansel Adams Center,
the primary benefit received by members of the
organization, emphasize contemporary photography yet are also
concerned with the criticism and history of the medium.
They include the newsletter* re:view, *the
periodic journal* Untitled *and major photographic monographs.
Membership is open to everyone. To receive
an informational membership brochure, write to Membership
Director, The Friends of Photography, Ansel Adams
Center, 250 Fourth Street, San Francisco, California 94103.*

COVER

Man Listening to Himself, 1988

Oil on silver print on canvas; 20" x 18½"
Courtesy of Ursula Gropper

Acknowledgements

This book is the fiftieth volume published by The Friends of Photography in its Untitled *series since 1972. In the past eighteen years, the series has addressed a wide range of subjects. It has included work by both contemporary and historical photographers and has presented a multiplicity of photographic genres and techniques.* Untitled I, *as the initial twenty-six-page book was simply called, contained an essay by Dody W. Thompson, "Edward Weston," along with a selection of the master's photographs. Perhaps no work could express the diversity of the* Untitled *series, as well as the dynamic progression of photography over the past two decades, than that contained in this present book.   Holly Roberts is a masterful artist who was first drawn to photography in search of subject matter for her drawings and lithographs. She soon discovered an affinity for the photographic image itself, as well as for painting, and the work included here is the result of a truly unique creative development over a period of seven years. This book serves as catalogue for an exhibition of Roberts' painted photographs held at the Ansel Adams Center in San Francisco from February 13 to April 22, 1990.   I would first like to thank Roberts for her enthusiastic assistance in all aspects of this project. Her willingness to share her work and her ideas allowed everything to go smoothly. I would also like to acknowledge all of the individuals and institutions who loaned their Roberts works for the exhibition and granted permission for the reproductions here. In addition, thanks go to the following for assisting in locating works to be included: Jayne H. Baum, of the Jayne H. Baum Gallery, New York; Linda Durham, of the Linda Durham Gallery, Santa Fe; Carol Ehlers, of the Ehlers Caudill Gallery, Chicago; Terry Etherton, of the Etherton/Stern Gallery, Tucson; and Jerry Zbiral, of the Collected Image, Chicago.   On the staff of The Friends of Photography, thanks go to Debra Heimerdinger, Ellen Manchester and Margaret Moulton for their suggestions for the essay, and to volunteers John Breeden, Jason Rowe and Carol Sheinkopf for their editorial assistance. Thanks also go to Michael Mabry for his wonderful design of the book.*   **DF**

Holly Roberts was formally trained in other media, yet the greater part of her recognition has come through the photographic community. In 1985, she received the Ferguson Grant from The Friends of Photography, and she was the recipient of Photographers' Fellowships from the National Endowment for the Arts in 1985 and 1987. She has been included in many group exhibitions of photographs with applied color throughout the country, and her work has been shown in a number of commercial galleries. The exhibition for which this book serves as catalogue is the first major assessment of a significant body of work that successfully and skillfully combines painting and photography.

This work poses an interesting dilemma for the viewer, particularly for those who might favor a more traditional approach to both media. Roberts is a painter, yet it is the photograph underlying the paint, even when it can scarcely be seen, that gives the work its intriguing, mysterious power. Drawing from the iconography of primitive art, particularly that of the Native American, Mexican and Hispanic cultures of the Southwest, where she lives, she creates paintings that address a broad range of human emotions.   Given the extent to which Roberts obscures the photographic aspect of her work with paint, it might seem unusual for it to have received such widespread attention in primarily photographic contexts, but the 150-year history of photography is rife with examples of blending the two media. These range from subtle embellishments of color to full-scale colorized transformations of black and white, and even color, prints.   The earliest daguerreotypes and ambrotypes often included details of jewelry or cosmetics enhanced with gold or rouge-colored paint, and albumen-print portraits of government dignitaries done by the Mathew Brady studio in Washington, D. C., had color applied to ties and other sartorial details. Other historical traditions of painting on photographs lie closer to the work presented in this book. Tintypes of the 1880s were frequently painted so heavily that the photographic images were completely covered, and even large historical portraits assumed to have been painted from life are often found to have a photograph, rather than a blank surface, beneath the paint.   In the early twentieth century, purists insisted on the monochromatic integrity of the photographic image, but throughout the period commercial portrait photographers tinted their work to compete more directly with the realism of the popular but more expensive painted portraits. Hand-tinting even found its way into the hobbyist world in mid-century, with kits of oil paints sold complete with black and white photographs ready to be transformed into a more complete, colorful reality.   As creative photography gained a surer foothold in the art world in the late 1960s and early 1970s, such hand-tinting became a widely accepted tool the artist might use to add color to work at a time when color photography was still suspect. While this work began as a careful coloring intended to bring a soft realism to the image, both more enthusiastic application techniques and distortions of true color quickly became accepted. It is ironic that the great interest in extensively painted photographs during the 1980s came at the same time that color photography itself was becoming more readily done by artists and acknowledged by the viewing public. It would be a mistake, however, to view Holly Roberts' work only in the context of traditions of hand-painting in photography.   During the past two decades, while combining photography and paint has become widely practiced, another, more important development has also occurred. In recent years, an increasing number of artists trained in other media have also turned to photography. Some have made straight-forward photographs as an alternative expressive statement, while others have incorporated photographic images into their work as a part of continuing creative explorations. It is with this group of artists using photography that Roberts, who trained in printmaking, drawing and painting before beginning her involvement with photography, has the greatest affinity.   Holly Roberts was born in 1951 in Boulder, Colorado, where her parents were students at the University of Colorado. Her family moved to Santa Fe, New Mexico, some three years later. After an accelerated high school career, Holly left home at sixteen to attend Western State College in Gunnison, Colorado, on a scholarship. She transferred to the University of California at Santa Barbara in 1970. In Santa Barbara she became involved in the radical politics and lifestyle of the campus community, but she never felt fully a part of the scene there. In 1971, needing a respite from that environment, she moved to Mexico and studied at the Belles Artes de Mexico in San Miguel de Allende. This was followed in 1972 by further study at the University of New Mexico's Andean Center in Quito, Ecuador.   Roberts' interest in printmaking evolved during the time she spent in Mexico and Ecuador. Upon returning to the United States, she enrolled at the University of New Mexico to study lithography, gaining her bachelor of arts degree in 1973. Following graduation, she worked as a curator at Tamarind Institute, the lithography school and workshop that had moved to Albuquerque from Los Angeles only a few years before. Her work at Tamarind involved assisting the invited artists who came to produce work there, and she was able to continue her own printmaking at the same time. She became disenchanted, however, because of the involved and indirect procedures that were required. She took several painting classes at the University and soon discovered that the relative immediacy of that medium better matched her creative temperament.

While in Albuquerque, she became reacquainted with Robert Wilson, whom she had known as a child in Santa Fe. In 1978, Wilson and Roberts moved to Tempe, Arizona, where he was to complete his medical residency. Roberts was accepted into the graduate program at Arizona State University. She initially enrolled as printmaker, but soon switched her major to drawing. She continued to paint actively while she was in school, receiving her master of fine arts degree in 1980. Two years later, Wilson was appointed to the Indian Health Service Hospital in Zuni, New Mexico, and the couple moved to Black Rock, the non-Indian support community on the Zuni Pueblo, where they live today.   Roberts' initial use of photographs in her work came not from an interest in the photographic image itself, but from a search for subject matter. In 1976, while she was still in Albuquerque, she began using pictures from magazines as the basis of drawings that were ultimately executed as prints. While this approach met her immediate needs, she decided she might as well work from her own photographs and enrolled in a photography class at the University. Some of the graduate students were hand-coloring their photographs, and Roberts experimented with this technique, but at the time it did not hold her attention. She next tried painting more heavily on the photographs and found she enjoyed working with them in that way. She continued to use her photographs as inspiration for her painting on canvas, but at the same time she experimented with creating painted photographs.   Roberts' first strong success at this process came in 1980. These pieces, like the earlier works, were essentially produced by painting "inside the lines," but by this time Roberts was completely taken by the possibilities of the technique. Instead of functioning as studies or sketches to be transposed into paintings or prints, the photographs now assumed a presence of their own, and the special nature of the photographic image became integrated within the work itself.   Key to this evolution was Roberts' realization that the photographic image that formed the substrate for the painting was always there; that it was unchanged and that she could do anything with the paint applied to its surface. In her early work, she used the paint to enhance parts of the photograph with color, marks and gestures, but still maintained the inherent visual integrity of the photograph.   Roberts feels that her primary effort in the early 1980s was in learning the craft and vocabulary of painting and becoming comfortable with the medium. She experimented with different methods of paint application such as bottle brushes, house-paint brushes and brayers. She also worked with different tools for marking the surface of the paint, ranging from palette knives to manicurists' orange sticks.   At the same time that she was developing her facility as a painter, Roberts was expanding her photographic repertoire. The photographs she utilized in her earliest painted works were straightforward, static compositions. She now began to use longer exposures and to move the camera or pan with moving objects within the frame. The resulting blurring of portions of the photograph allowed Roberts to make a creative leap that moved her work forward significantly. The blurred forms became departure points that hinted at or suggested other image possibilities that could be brought forward as the paint was applied.   The images made after 1983 have a different, more fluid, quality. With the underlying photograph less distinct, Roberts was able to direct the content of the painting by creating elements such as arms, legs and heads, changing the relative scale of body parts and introducing objects that did not appear in the original photograph at all. This new freedom strongly affected the work of the next several years; it is clearly seen in paintings done in 1984. One could argue, of course, that Roberts would have had the same freedom had she done her painting on blank canvas, but she insists that raw canvas would give her nothing to break free from, that by starting with the picture, her painting becomes a kind of record of a unique interaction between artist, photograph and paint.   This connection to the photograph is both critical to Roberts' aesthetic and key to understanding her paintings. Like all artists, Roberts has made shifts in direction that proved unsuccessful yet gave her a greater insight into what she was doing. One of these is particularly interesting for its reinforcement of the primacy of the photographic aspects of her work. At some point after she began to move the content of the painting away from the direct subject of the photograph, Roberts decided that, since she was painting with such freedom, perhaps the specific photograph she used did not matter. She went out and made exposures of the ground itself, of sticks and stones and dirt. She found little on her proof sheet that motivated her, and even though she did make one painting that she liked from the group, the process of doing it was so lifeless that she abandoned the approach. It was clear that the photograph *did* matter.   A different kind of technical understanding came several years later, in 1986, when Roberts began cutting shaped portions of her photographs and mounting them on a larger pieces of canvas. This not only allowed her to work on a larger scale, but it also introduced a complexity of surface quality and texture, since the paint sits differently on the smooth surface of the silver print than it does on the rougher fabric. The technique also enabled her to combine parts of more than one photographic image on the canvas, so that her painting was done as a reaction to a newly created photographic image.   Even though Roberts liked the results of the paintings with photographs collaged onto canvas, she did not abandon her work with single, complete photographic prints. In recent years, she has continued both approaches. Throughout her career, Roberts has slowly increased the size of her work. The earliest pieces are done on eight by ten-inch paper; the most recent are as large as thirty by forty inches. The decision to combine photographs on canvas in part came from wanting to make larger paintings, in fact. To get the scale she now desires in the work done on photographs alone, she stopped using boxed photographic paper that holds her to sizes determined by the manufacturer and began to make her prints on rolled mural paper. Unlike the traditional photographer, for whom moving to a larger size means only an adjustment of printing controls, for Roberts, each step larger requires a rethinking of the way in which the paint is applied and worked on the surface as well as an extension of the time required to complete a piece.   The content of Holly Roberts' images comes from two broad sources. First is her nearly life-long experience of living in the American Southwest, from an attachment not only to the colors of the landscape and its active, outdoor lifestyle, but to the ubiquitous influence of Native American, Mexican and Hispanic peoples indigenous to the area. The second source, which gets closer to the meaning of her work, is a conceptualization of human emotions, cultural history and interpersonal relationships. These sources are clearly not mutually exclusive, of course. The images that include horses, deer, birds and other animals frequently reflect the emotional concerns of the other works, and those concerned more directly with emotion are similarly peopled by figures that might be found in the stories of her Zuni neighbors.   Roberts chooses not to talk about the reactive process she goes through to reach her final image. She also dislikes discussing what her paintings are about, feeling that her involvement is completed once the piece is finished, and that a viewer's experience with it is determined by what he or she brings to it. Similarly, Roberts is particularly drawn to the visual arts, but insists she is not interested in critical ideas about them. Rather, she is interested in the visual presence of the artworks, in their inherent power and in the physicality of the objects themselves.   If enlightenment cannot come from Roberts' words, perhaps the viewer can gain insight from a catalogue of her admitted interests in the arts. Influences from Zuni and Southwest Indian art are clearly a part of Roberts' imagery, but she also acknowledges an interest in the art of indigenous cultures throughout the world. She speaks of the commonality of all of these influences on her, not just of those from Zuni. She is particularly drawn to the kachinas and fetishes of the Pueblo Indians, as well as to Mexican Masks, Hispanic religious art and the carvings of Pacific Northwest groups. From the past, she is fascinated by Mimbres pottery, petroglyphs and pictographs from the Southwest—such as those from Horseshoe Canyon in Southern Utah—and very early Egyptian art.   Roberts' influences are not only from primitive art, of course, and the influences she most identifies with at any time change as her work develops. Among painters, she has been especially attracted to Edgar Degas, Henri de Toulouse-Lautrec, Georgia O'Keeffe and Anselm Kiefer. She likes the simplicity inherent in David Hockney's painting and the emotion in that of Joan Brown, Francisco Clemente, Francis Bacon and Frida Kahlo.   In photography, she has a great appreciation for the work of Diane Arbus, feeling that Arbus had a respect and admiration for her subjects as well as a sense of compassion in her photography. She likes the otherness of Ralph Eugene Meatyard's photographs and what she sees as an unpretentious simplicity in the work of Garry Winogrand.   In literature, Roberts tends toward writers with poetic, darkly romantic visions—Günther Grass, Gabriel García Marquez, Anne Tyler—and those investigating alternative realities—Carlos Castenada and Stanislav Groff, particularly his book *Human Encounter with Death.* The fact that her list of authors has no historical figures accentuates the primacy of her involvement with the visual arts. Roberts feels that one can look at a petroglyph incised in a rock wall and have a religious, emotional experience approximating that of its makers, but that one cannot have the same exprience with a book written one hundred years ago.

The diversity of these influences provides an insight into the mix of ideas that informs Roberts' own creative work. Many viewers of Roberts' work, keying in on the fact of Roberts' residence in Zuni, perceive only the connections to Southwest cultures. While some images contain figures that are clearly patterned after those seen in dances and art objects of Southwest cultures, and other of her figures resemble those seen in pictographs and petroglyphs, Roberts is clearly drawn in a more general sense to primitive art.   Stick-like appendages, flattened space and the transformation of human and animal forms are elements in Roberts' work that are found in functional and aesthetic objects from throughout the world. Her striving for simplicity within the images and her use of figures internally charged with meaning but freed from an enveloping environment are other aspects of this borrowing. Like Roberts, countless artists of the past century have found inspiration in indigenous objects, and it is instructive that such objects, even though they may not have been created for aesthetic purposes, can transcend the purposes of their makers and find a spiritual home within contemporary Western art. For Roberts, the utilization of figures influenced by primitive art provides a ready path for exploring elemental relationships and emotions.   In addition to the maturation of painting style and visualization of the paintings from 1984, Roberts' work from that year also shows the emergence of a more personal vision. Most of her prior imagery had contained objectified figures, such as *Bob with Mask* (Plate 1), *Man With Iguana* and *Deer's Head* (Plate 3). The emotional content of the paintings became more complex as Roberts took on a clear concern with events and relationships surrounding her. Paintings such as *Leaving Phoenix* (Plate 6) give more emotional weight to recent events from her life, although the actual move had taken place two years before. Perhaps more indicative of this shift in her work are *Being Distressed* (Plate 12) and *Bob as Blackie* (Plate 4), which deal with her response to aspects of her husband's life. The first of these was done in response to his grieving over the deaths of several children in his medical practice; the second portrays the psychic unity between Bob and his dog. *Bob as Blackie* is one of the first expressions of a concept that rises again and again in Roberts' work, that of one person presented as someone or something else, as being inside another figure. And with work such as this it becomes clear that Roberts' use of elements from primitive art is not just an appropriation, but the incorporation of a sense of spirit that is essentially absent in Western culture.

Following her breakthrough year of 1984, Roberts continued to work with intensified emotions, but more frequently without the specific references to the personal experiences of her family. The images are objectified once again, but they contain more universal references to emotions: *Woman Being Angry* (Plate 19), *Nothing Sexual* and *Man Being Modest* (Plate 22). These images are more and more direct, with a figure or figures placed against a non-specific background, often addressing the viewer in a confrontational manner rather than being involved in actions within the frame.   This separation of the figures from a specific environment is carried into the most recent work presented in this book, but now in an even different manner. Paintings such as *Woman on Fire* (Plate 36) and *Woman Dancing on Top of a Hill* (Plate 37) appear to represent a purely spiritual plane. The figures in these archetypal images float within the painted surface. They exude light and energy, as if they represent a psychic transformation or an out-of-body experience.   In addition to illustrating how far Roberts' vision has evolved, *Woman Dancing on Top of a Hill* also shows how much her use of an underlying photograph has continued to be a part of her creative process. Compared to her earliest works, in which the paint was added to embellish the photograph, *Woman Dancing* comes from a truly remarkable melding of intellect, emotion and vision. The photograph Roberts used for this piece depicts the skeleton of a coyote lying in the desert; portions of it can be clearly seen along one edge. One can only speculate what kind of process Roberts went through to get from a macabre picture such as this to an image of such spiritual enlightenment.   Since moving to Zuni in 1982, Roberts has developed a very specific routine that allows her to both mix and separate her career as an artist and her involvement with family and community. She divides the year into two five-month working periods, taking time off between them. During these periods she paints regularly, sometimes photographing and making the prints to be used for future paintings. The intense creative activity is relieved by attention given to the business side of being an artist—correspondence, gallery dealings, sorting and filing slides and traveling for lectures and workshops.

Roberts' painting is done in a room at one end of the forty-foot mobile home she rents from one of their Zuni neighbors; Bob's smaller sculpture studio is at the other end; the darkroom is in the center of the structure. In the portions of the year when she is working, Roberts completes her morning household tasks, feeds her two horses and takes her daughter to the babysitter before arriving in her studio in early afternoon. Once her preparations are complete—this may take an hour or two— she begins to work, continuing until the painting is completed, which may be as late as 11 p.m. This approach is necessitated by her preference of working on a wet surface, of always painting wet paint into wet paint. Although she sometimes will work on a painting over two days in the winter, the summertime heat in New Mexico dries the paint too quickly. The demands of this routine have, of course, become greater over the years as the paintings have become progressively larger.   One of the surprising sights a viewer familiar with the subtle colors of Roberts' paintings finds upon visiting her studio is her palette, which is covered with mounds of very bright, pure colors. Once she has selected the photograph or photo/canvas collage to be worked on, one that she feels will provide the necessary emotional trigger for the work to proceed that day, Roberts applies the separate oil paints directly onto the surface, using her hands as well as printmaking brayers to spread and mix the paint. As the image she conceives begins to take shape in her mind, she uses brushes to shape it, applying additional color to develop specific forms or to make areas darker or lighter, or scratches the surface of the paintng to etch outlines of figures or make gestural marks.   What appears as her preference for a grayed palette comes, then, from a mixing of colors. In part, the movement from brighter, more distinct colors in her early work to the grayer tones of her recent pieces comes as much from the increased working of the paint as the pieces became larger as it does from her maturing of style. It is striking how closely the coloration of Roberts' work matches that of the Southwestern landscape. Despite the intense sunlight of the region and the monumental nature of its geologic features, the tone of much of the land is subtle and subdued. Except for a bright blue, high-altitude sky, the colors of the landscape tend toward the grayer, subtler hues. Shortly after moving to Zuni, in fact, as an exercise in establishing the color vocabulary of her style, Roberts took watercolors into the surrounding countryside to learn how to recreate those distinct colors. The hues that ultimately color Roberts' paintings are earthy and warm, and frequently tend toward the red. Accents of brighter colors abound, but, like the land of the Southwest, greens that are not muted are rare.   Throughout the process of painting, Roberts has a continuing interaction with the photographic image she is using, but unlike the interaction a traditional easel painter might have with a still life arrangement, for example, Roberts' is a process in constant transition. Each stroke of her brush and each added color change what she can see of the photograph, and this in turn changes the visual and emotional response that leads to the next stroke. Because of the smooth surface of the photographic print, Roberts can easily manipulate the amount of the photograph that is visible in the work throughout the entire painting process. She can wipe paint from the surface to allow certain areas of the photographic image to come through, or apply more to obscure unwanted detail.   The extent that Roberts covers or reveals her underlying photograph changes the degree of photographic presence in a particular work and the nature of the visual interplay between the two media. What gives her work such haunting power is the result of an elementary physiological fact: the mind processes photographic information differently than it does painted forms. Even a contemporary awareness of the constructed artifice of a photographic image cannot deny that a camera photographs something that existed. We relate the photographed object to the object itself. The painted forms, while also a creation of the artist, come from the world of the imagination. In paintings such as *Man Listening to Himself* (cover), in which the photograph is given nearly equal emphasis as the paint, the resonance of this dichotomy is clearly apparent. In works such as *Woman Dancing on Top of a Hill*, in which a smaller amount of photographic information is visible, and that contradictory to the painted figures, the viewer is moved to imply what cannot be seen and to feel the experience of the artist. While it is Roberts' evolving interaction with the photograph that takes her to her finished work, it is the existence of the underlying photographic image—even when it is obscured by paint—that gives the work its powerful qualities and sets up the emotional challenge for the viewer.

by David Featherstone

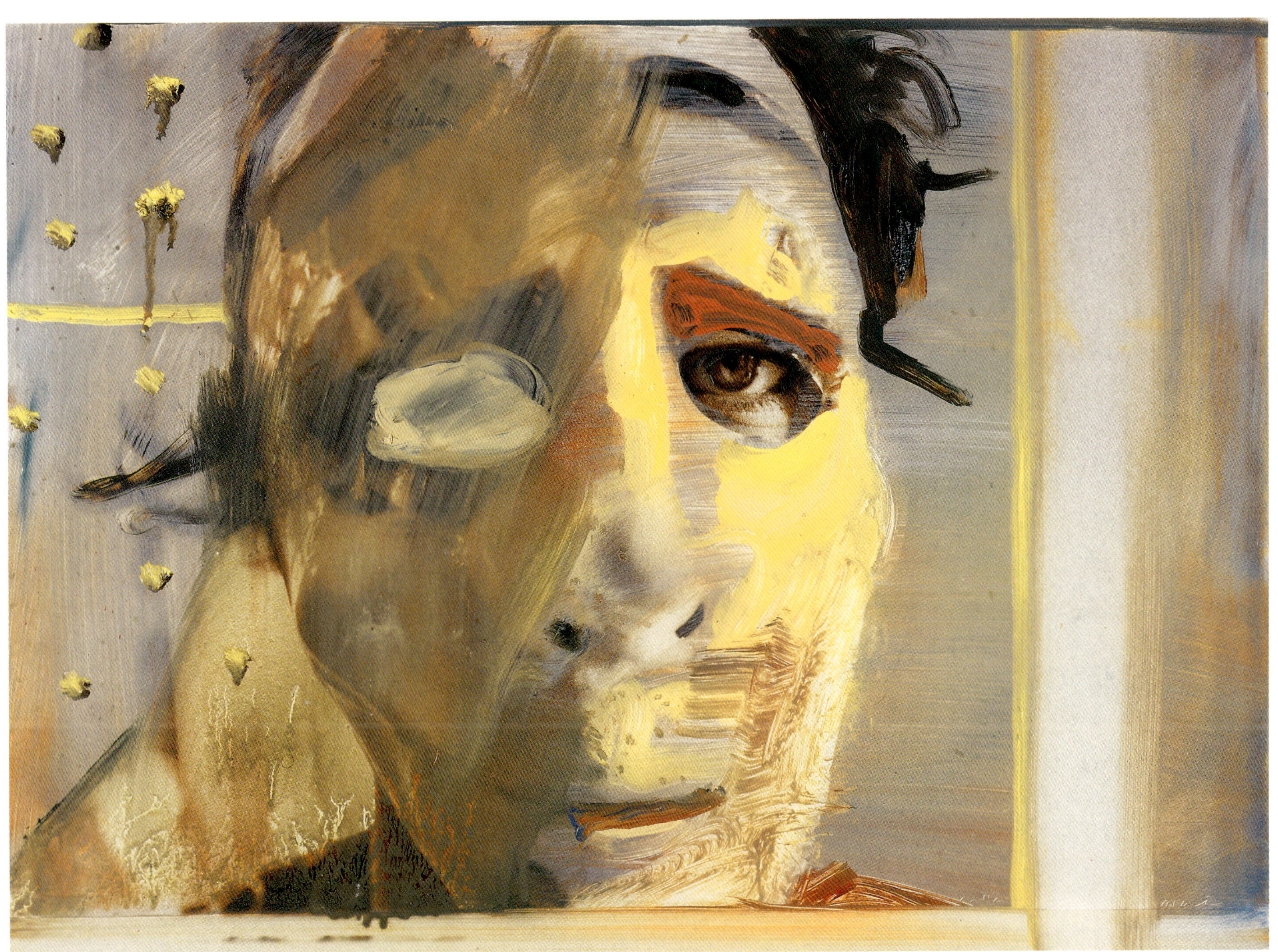

PLATE I
Bob with Mask 1982
Oil on silver print; 16" x 20"
Courtesy of J. J. Brookings Gallery, Timothy C. Duran, Director

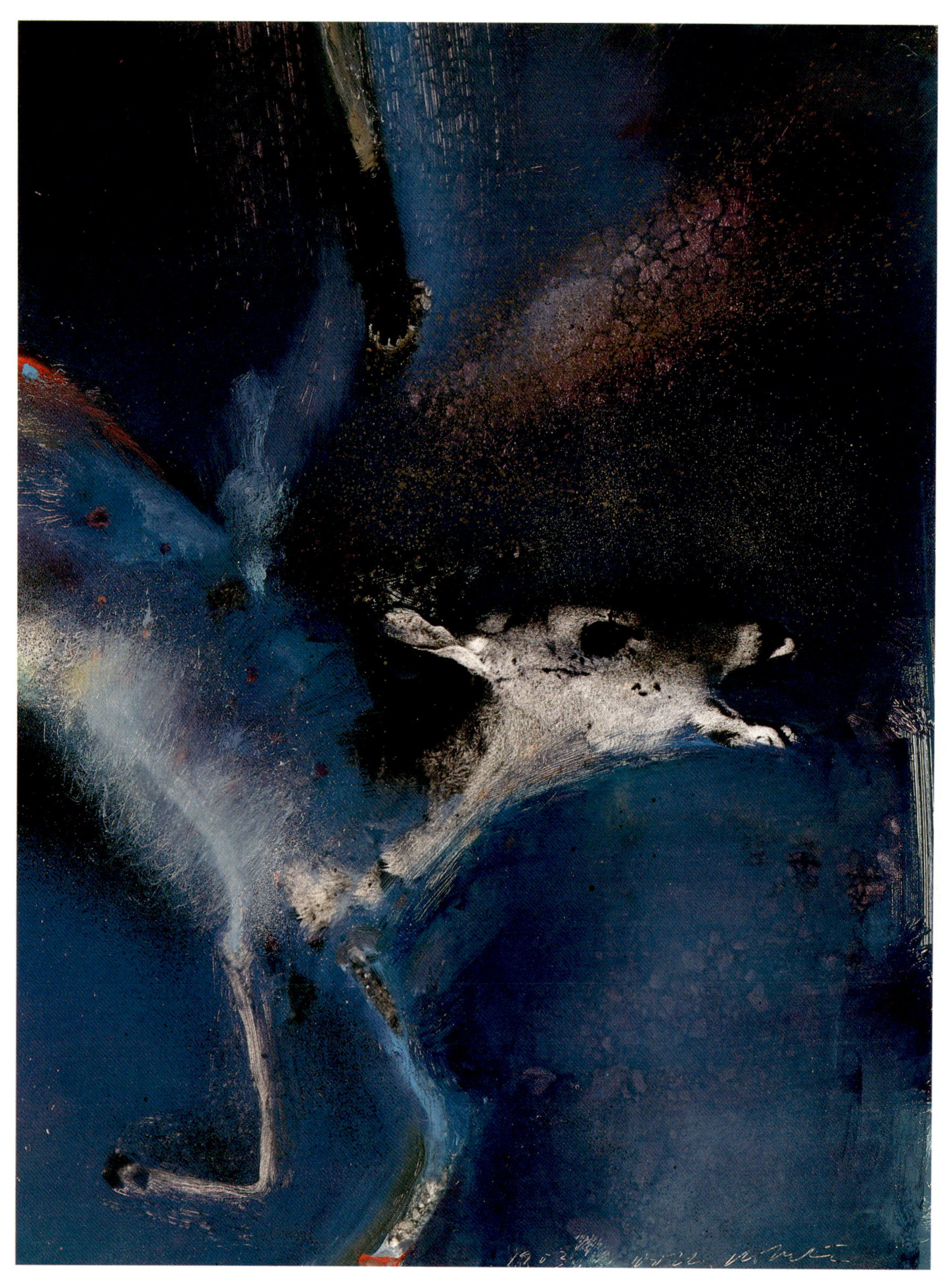

PLATE 2
Deer with Paw, 1983
Oil on silver print; 18 ¾" x 14¼"
Courtesy of the artist

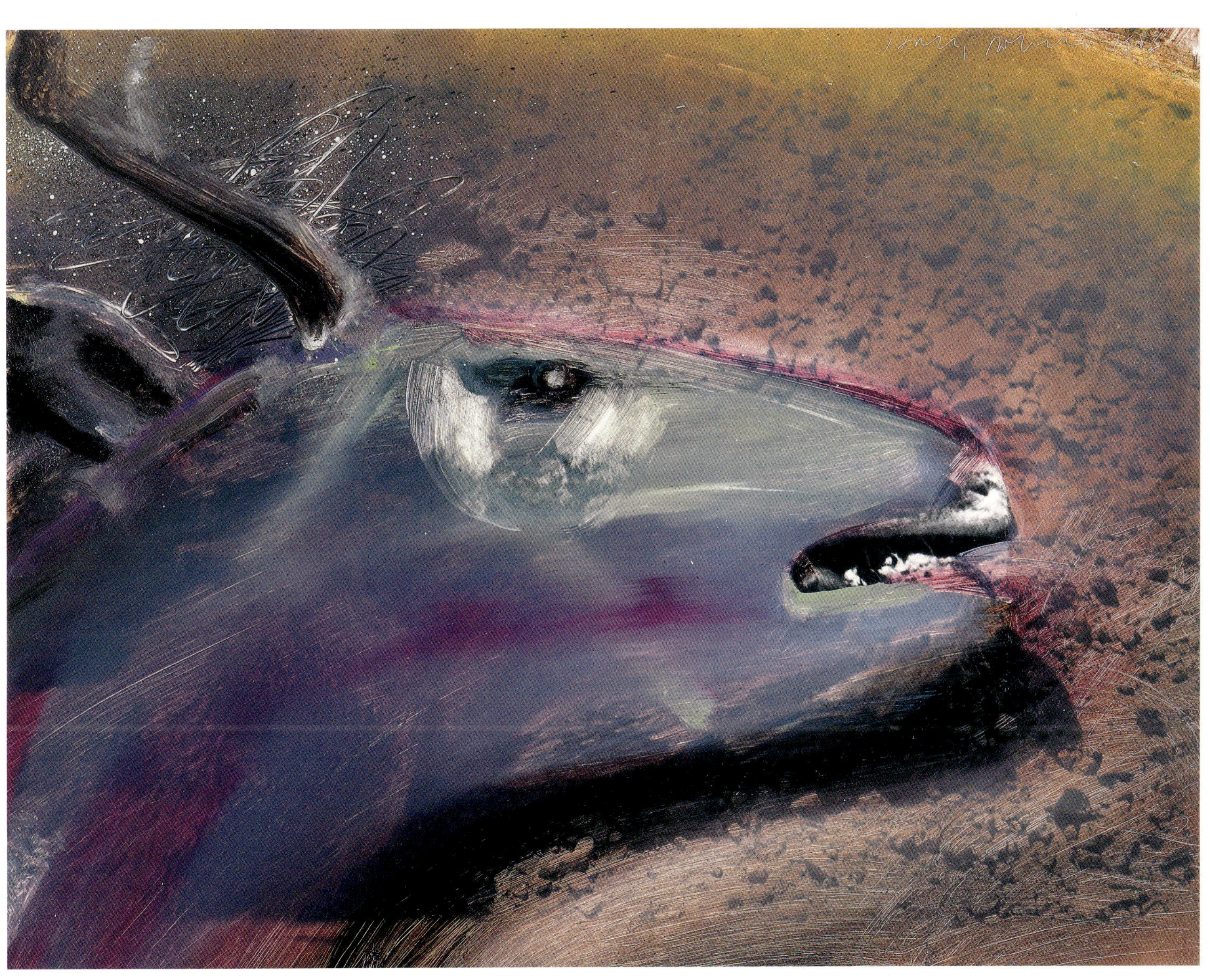

PLATE 3

Deer's Head, 1983

Oil on silver print; 16" x 20"

Courtesy of Linda Connor

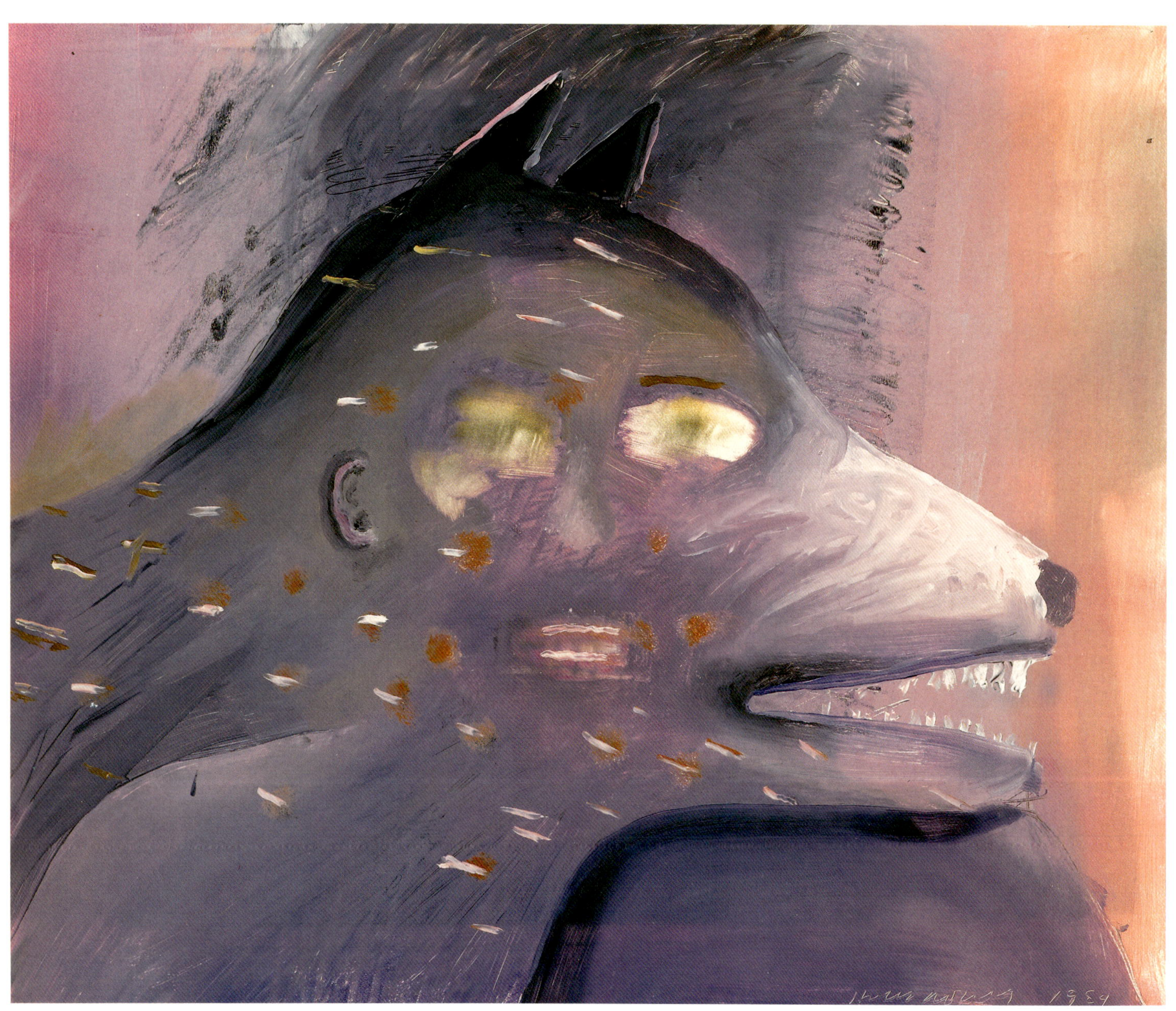

PLATE 4

Bob as Blackie, 1984

Oil on silver print, 20" x 24"

Courtesy of Pamela Portwood and Mark Taylor

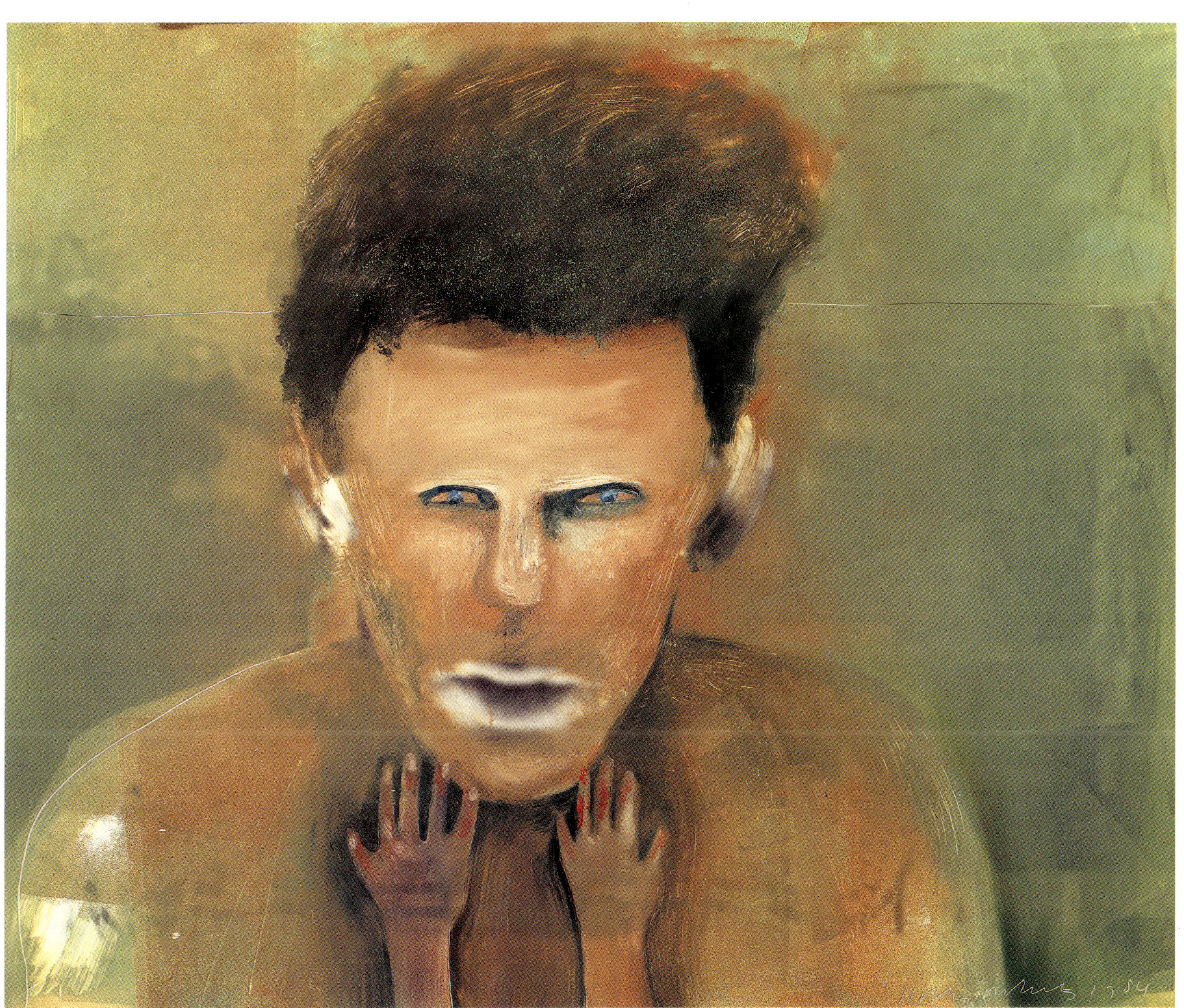

PLATE 5

Bob with Small Hands, 1984

Oil on silver print; 18¼" x 22½"

Courtesy of the artist

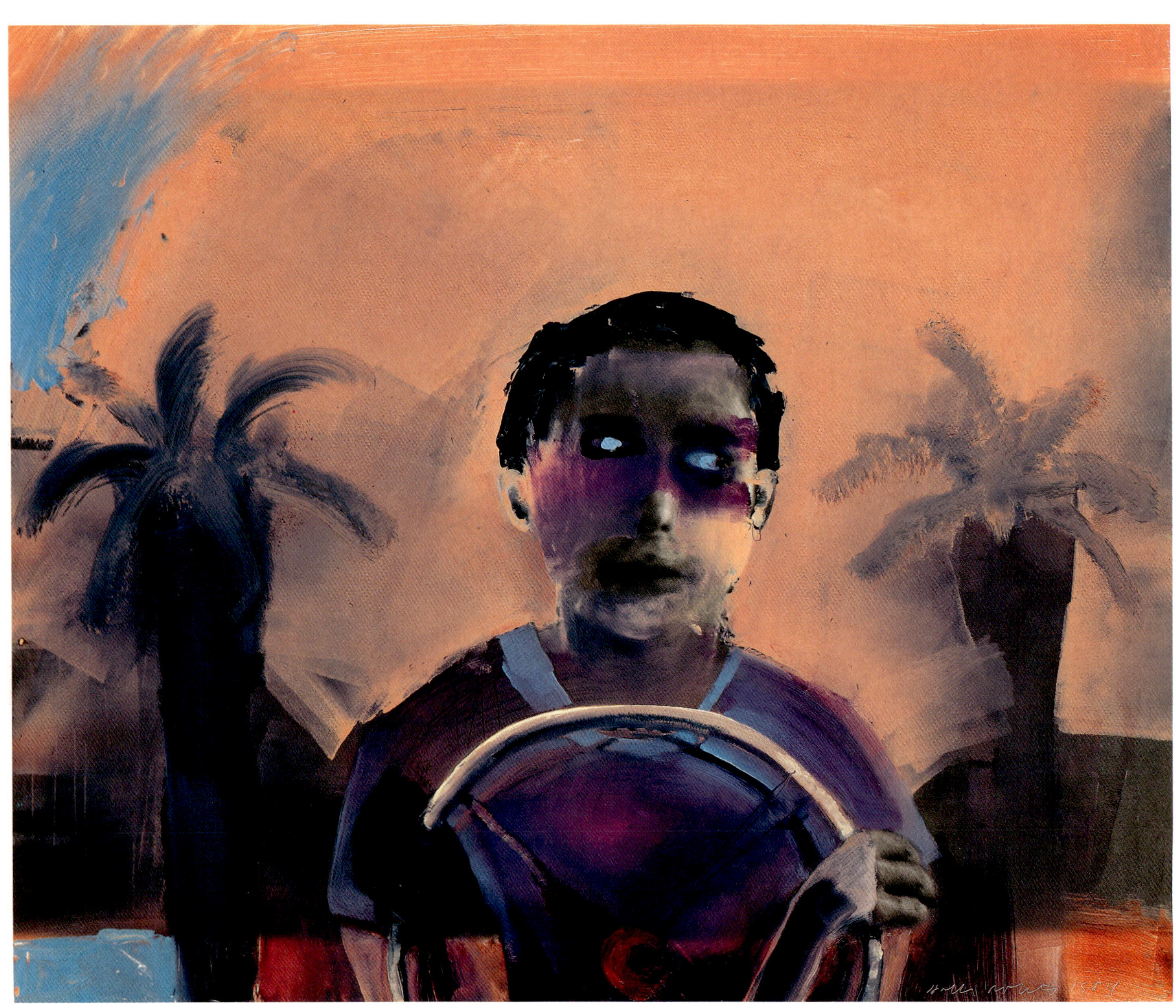

PLATE 6
Leaving Phoenix, 1984
Oil on silver print; 18¼" x 22½"
Courtesy of the artist

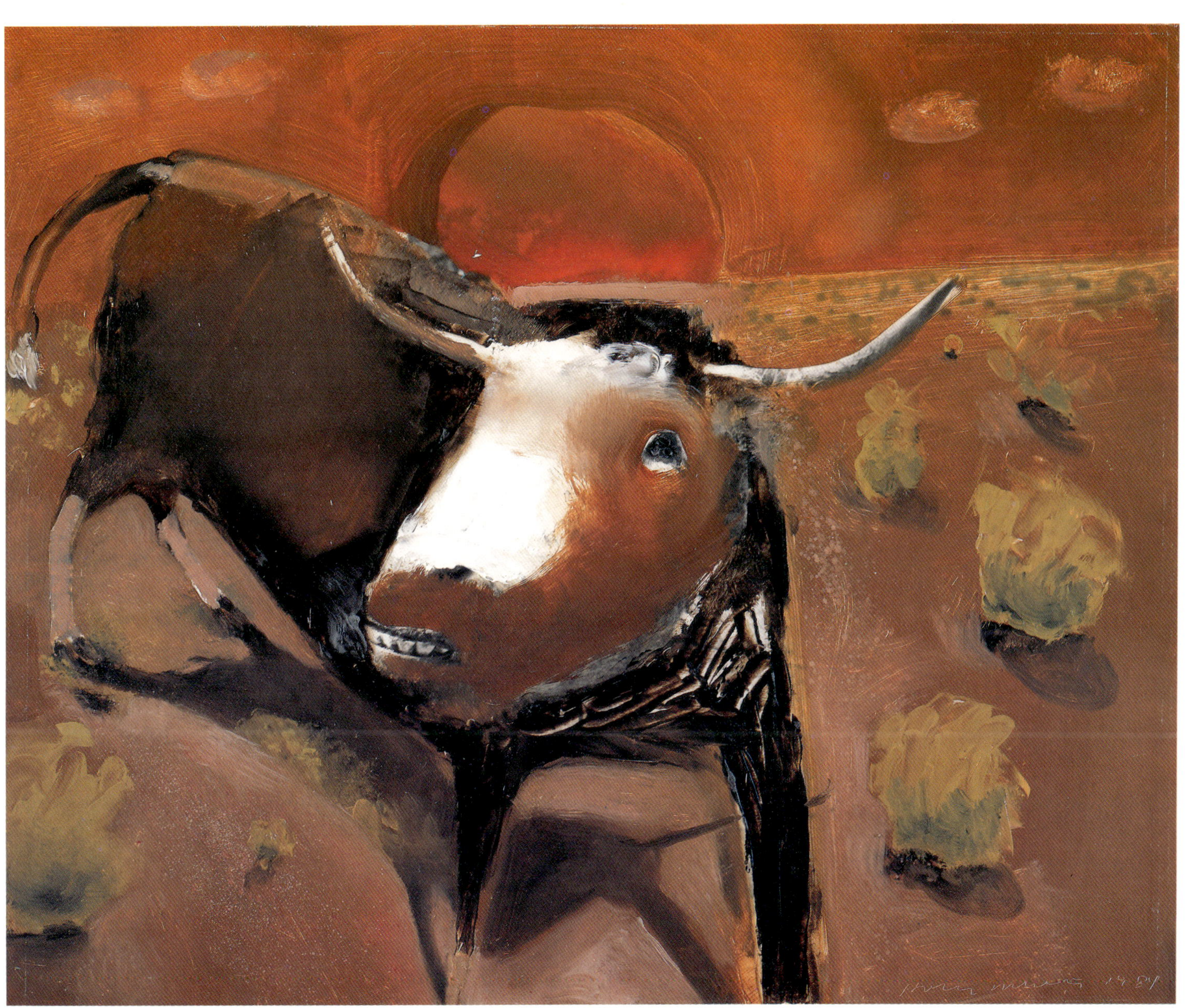

PLATE 7

Steer, 1984

Oil on silver print; 20" x 24"

Private collection

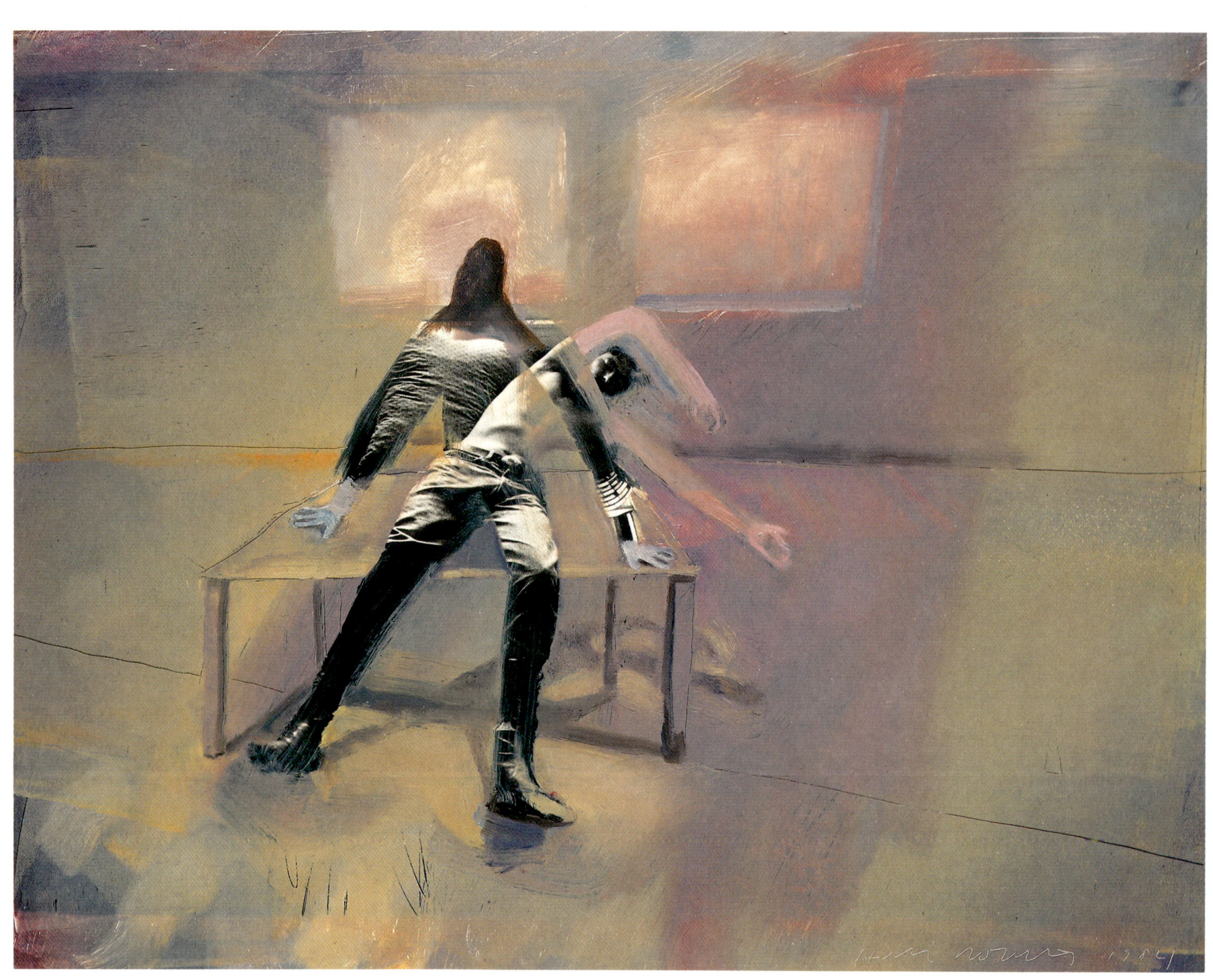

Bob Dreaming, 1984
Oil on silver print; 14¼" x 18¾"
Courtesy of the artist

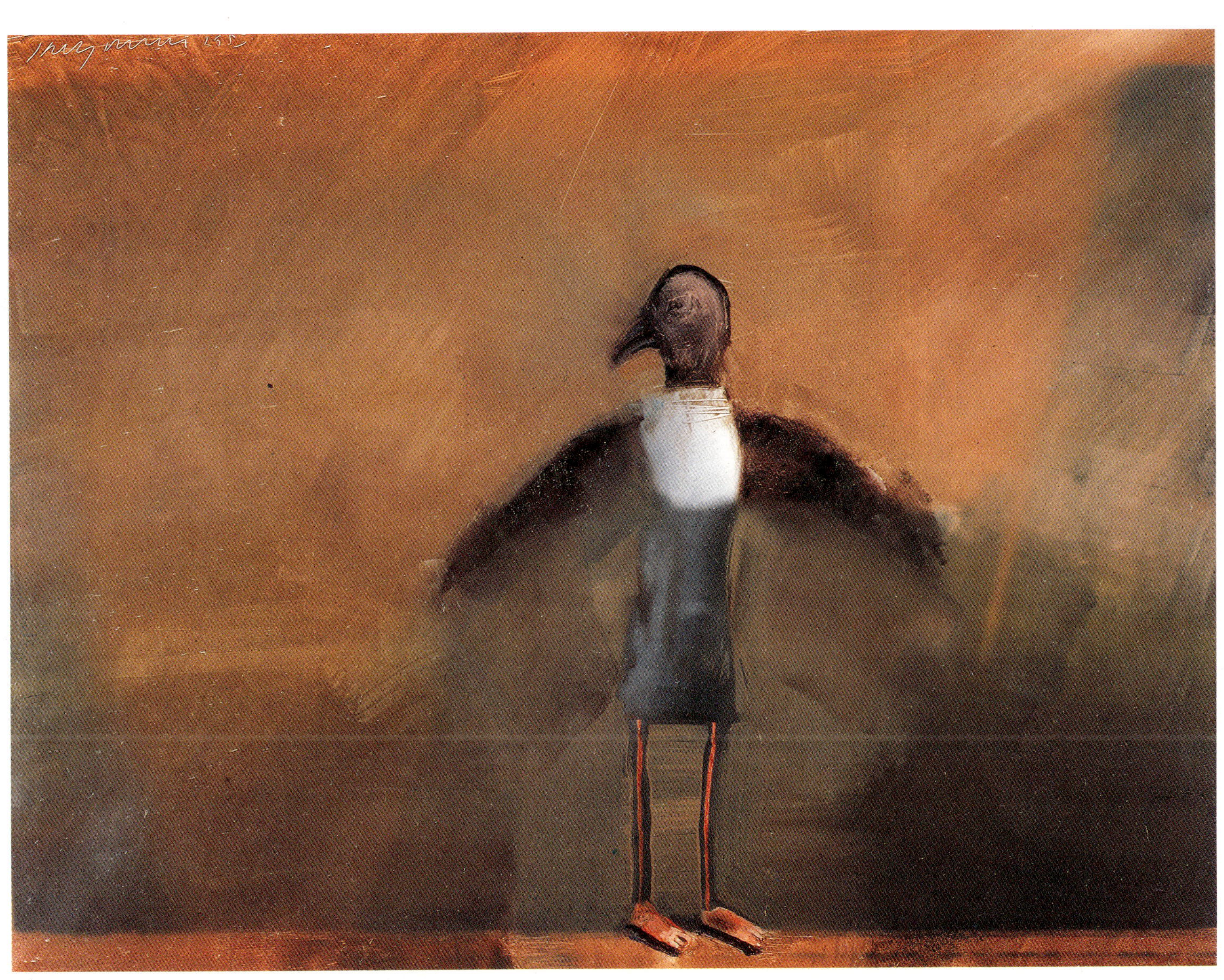

PLATE 9
Small Bird, 1985
Oil on silver print; 14 ⅜" x 19"
Museum of Fine Arts, Museum of New Mexico
Gift of Linda Durham, 1987

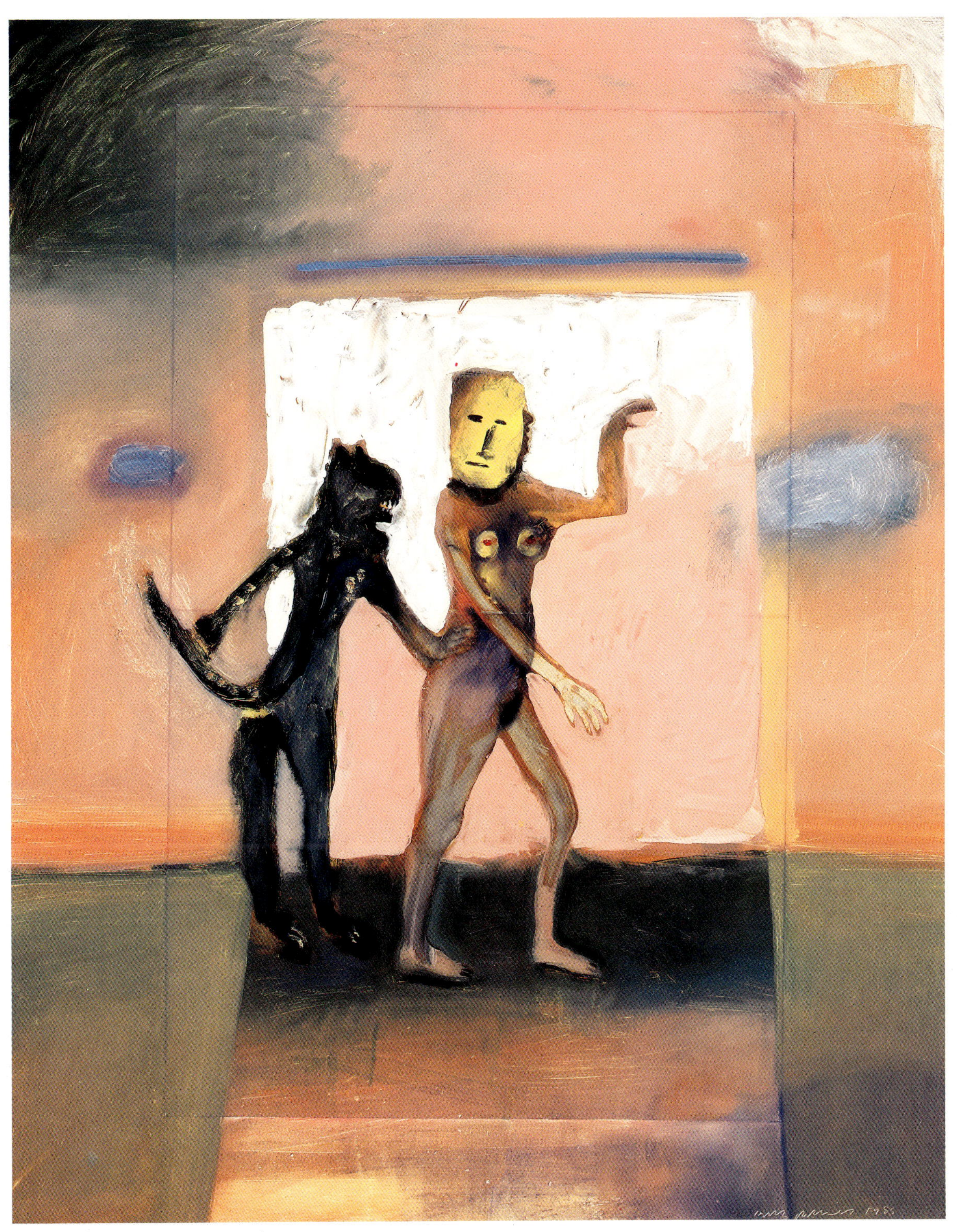

PLATE 10

Woman with Mountain Lion, 1985

Oil on silver print on paper; 40" x 30"

Courtesy of the artist

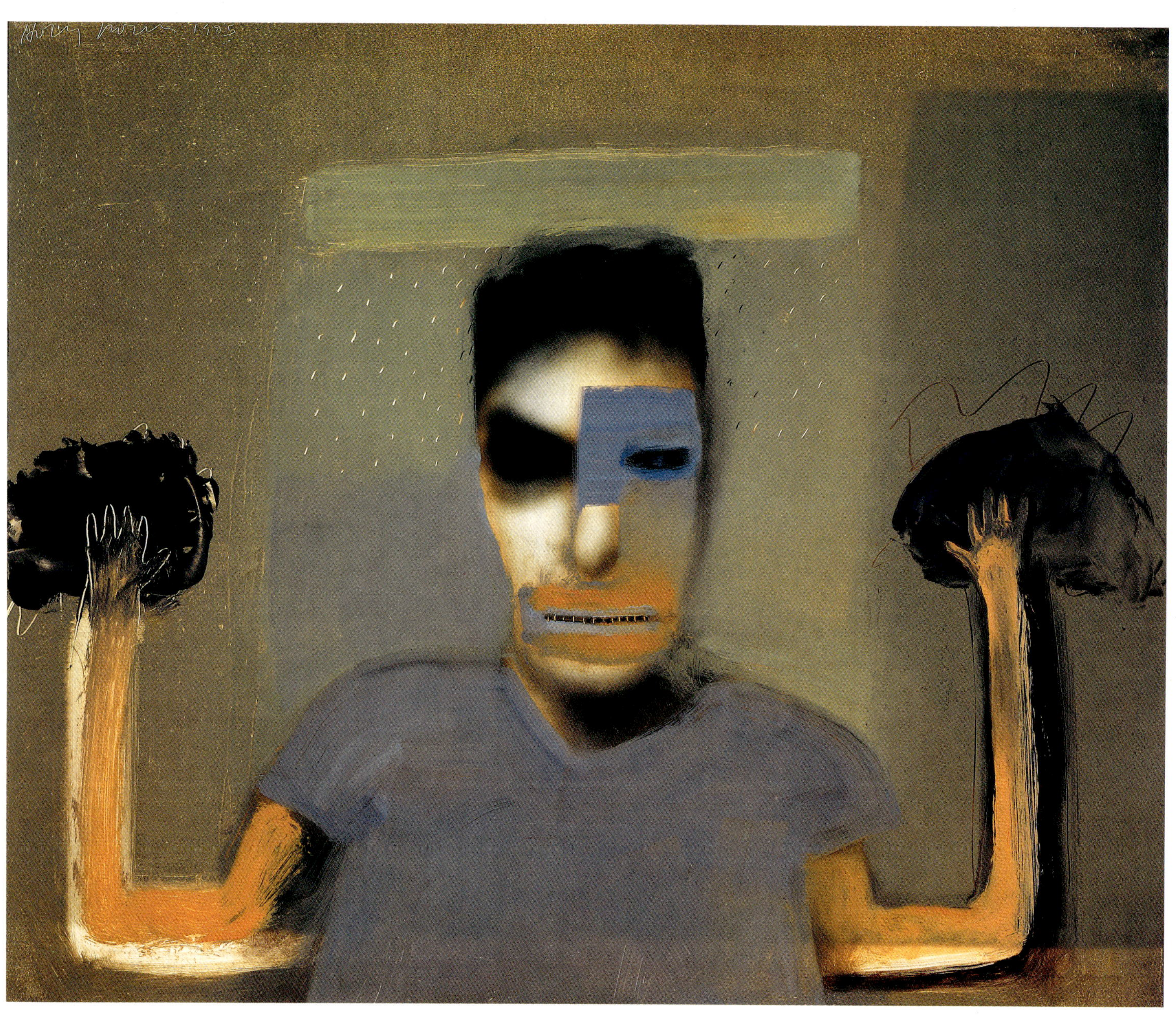

PLATE II
Praying for Rain, 1985
Oil on silver print; 20" x 24"
86.200. Collection of the University Art Museum,
University of New Mexico, Albuquerque

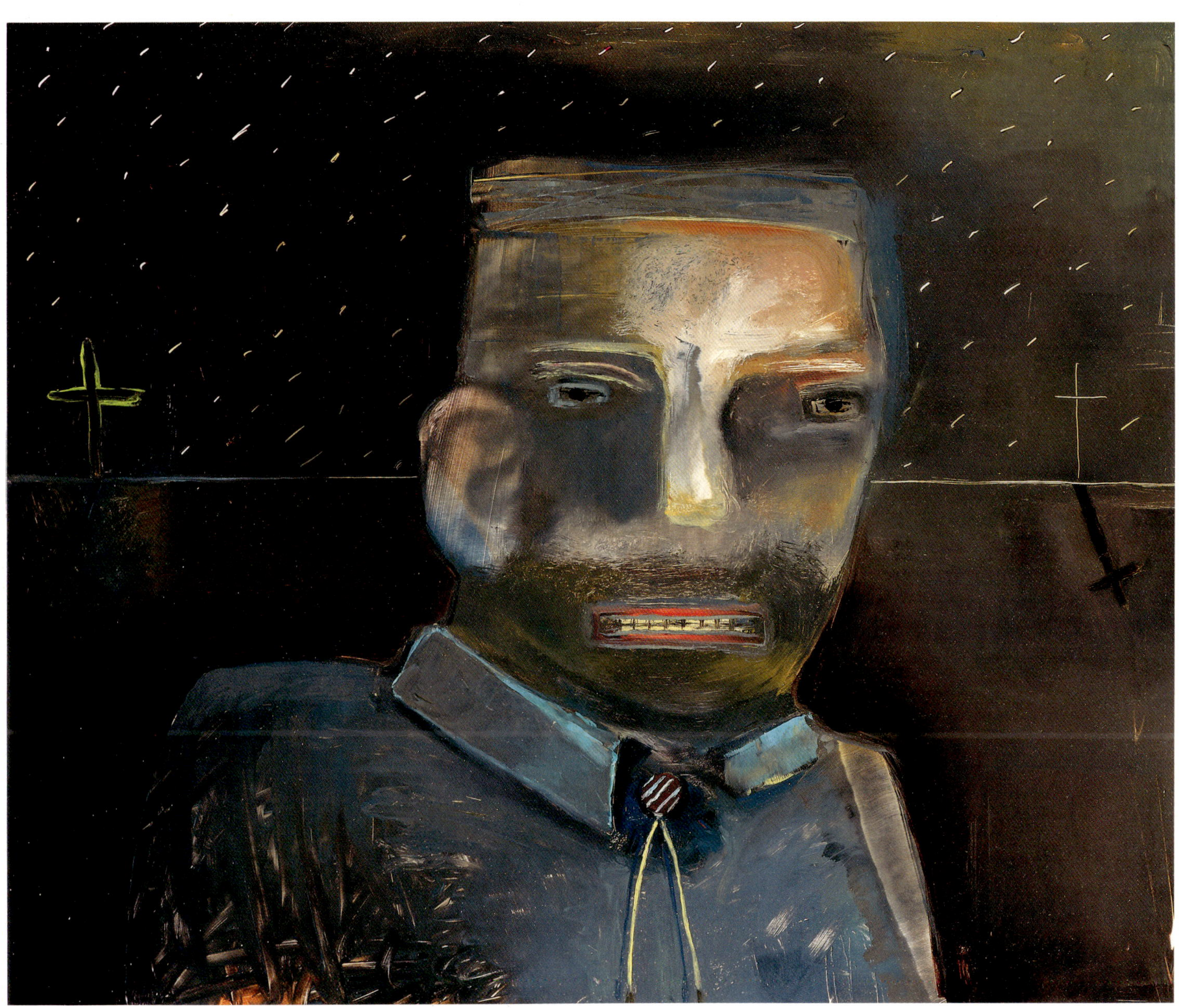

PLATE 12

Being Distressed, 1985

Oil on silver print; 18¼" x 22½"

Courtesy of the artist

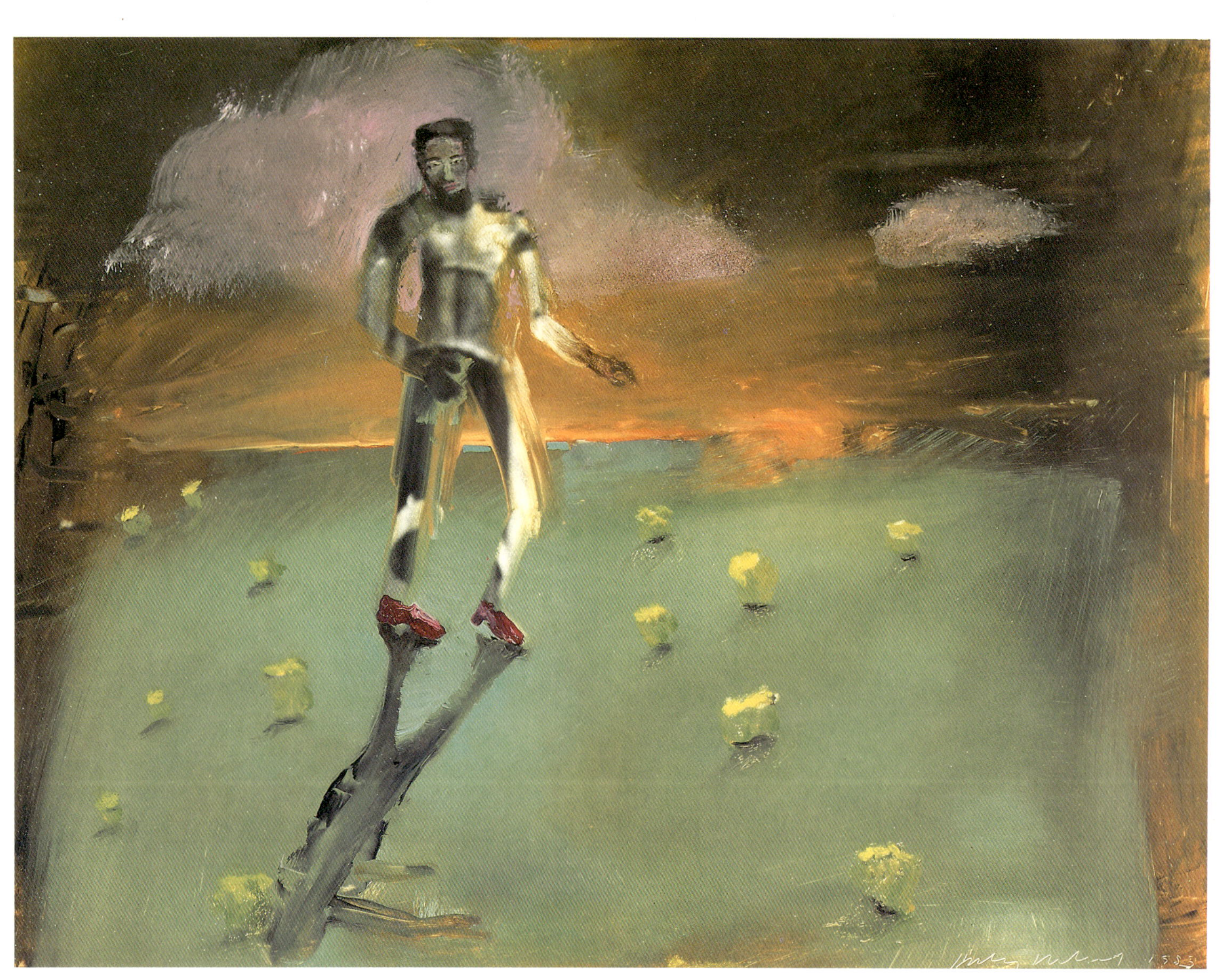

PLATE 13
Man in the Desert, 1985
Oil on silver print; 16" x 20"
Courtesy of Helle Mathiasen

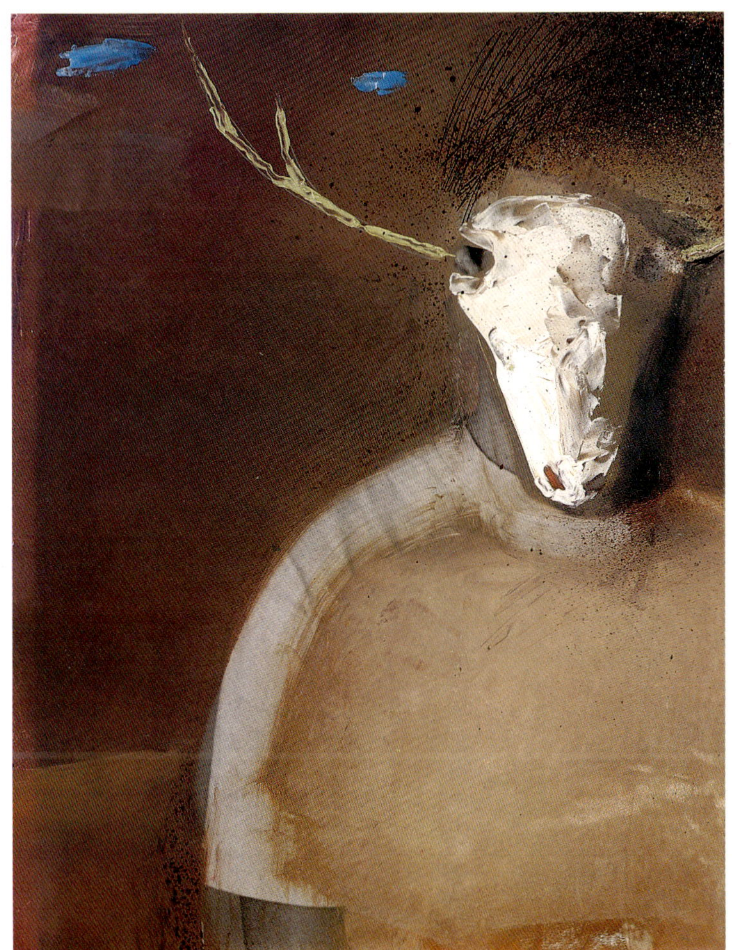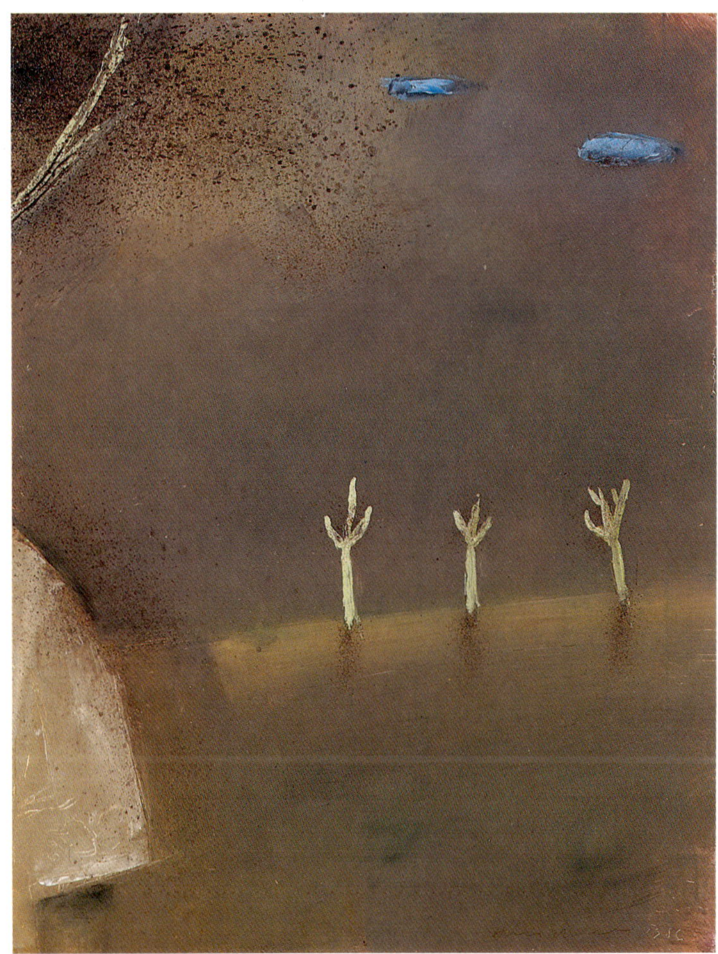

PLATE 14
Bob with Deer Mask, 1986
Oil on silver print; 20" x 32"
Courtesy of Bruce Johnson and Mary Laukes Johnson

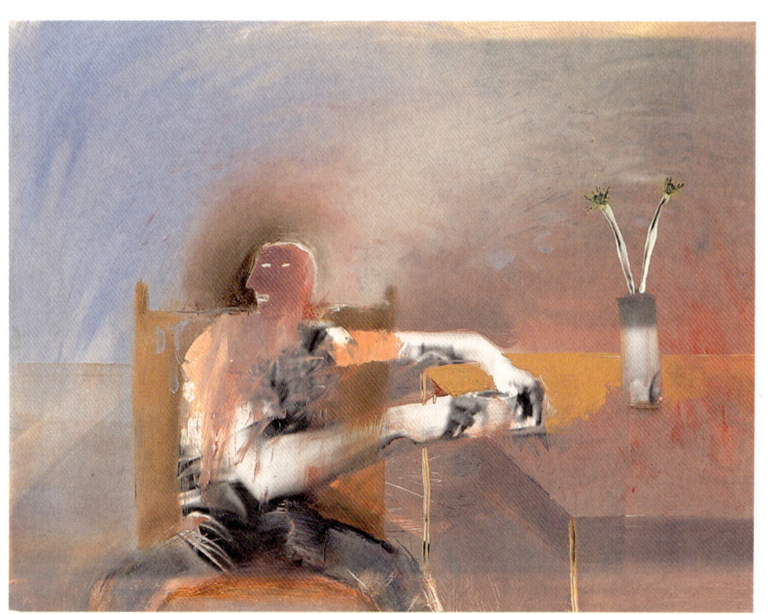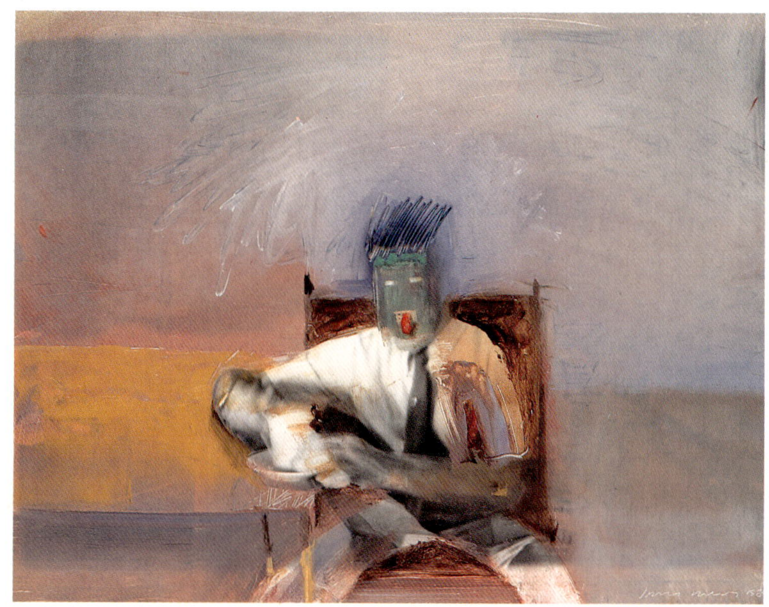

PLATE 15
Two Men Having Tea, 1986
Oil on silver print; 16" x 40"
Courtesy of Terry and Mary Ellen Etherton

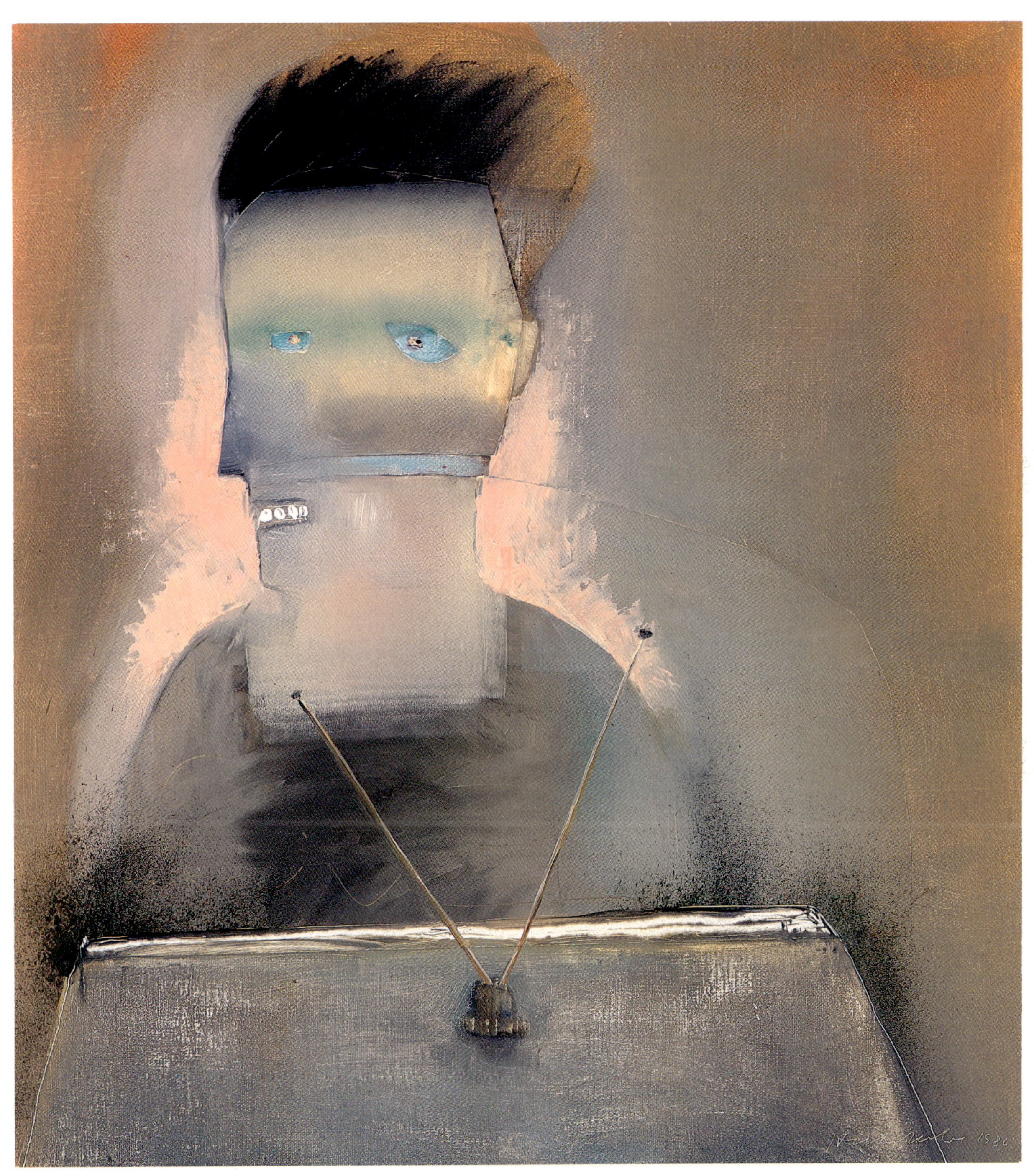

PLATE 16

Man with T.V., 1986

Oil on silver print on canvas; 21" x 19"

Courtesy of the artist

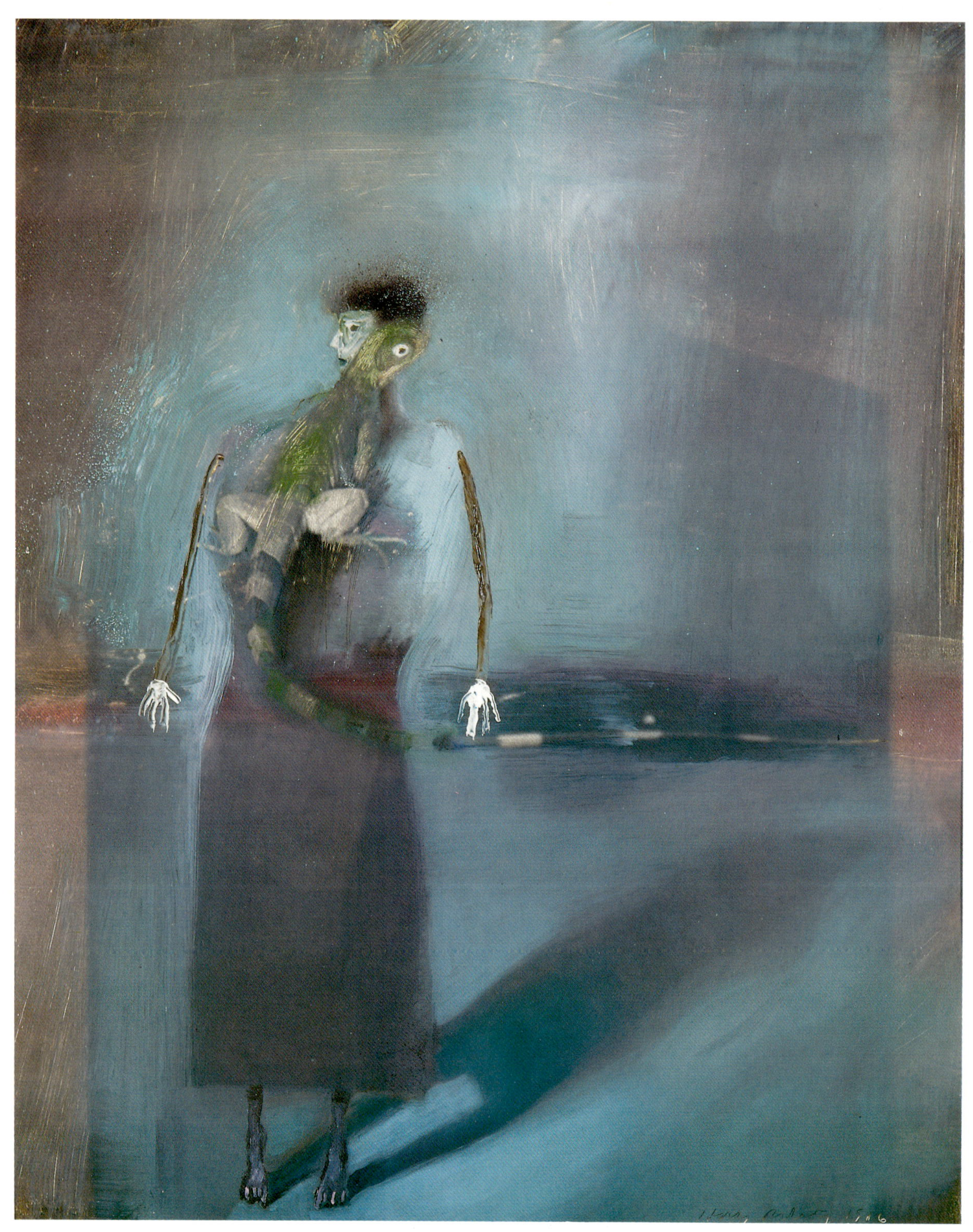

PLATE 17
Woman with Lizard, 1986

Oil on silver print; 24" x 20"
Courtesy of Sharon Louise Lane

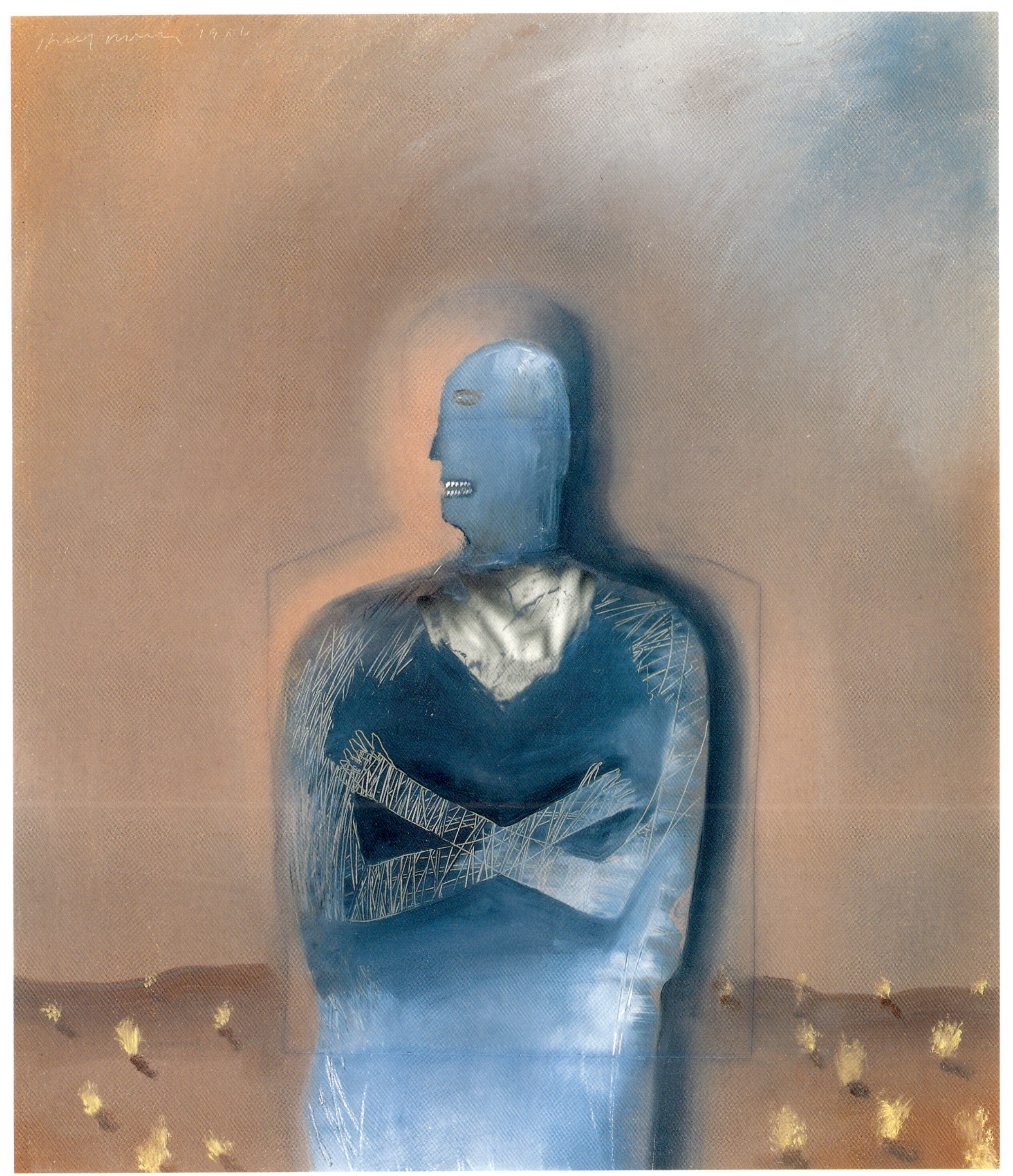

PLATE 18
Being Alone in the Desert, 1986
Oil on silver print; 24" x 21"
Museum of Fine Arts, Museum of New Mexico
Purchased with funds donated by Mel and Dickie Pfaelzer, 1986

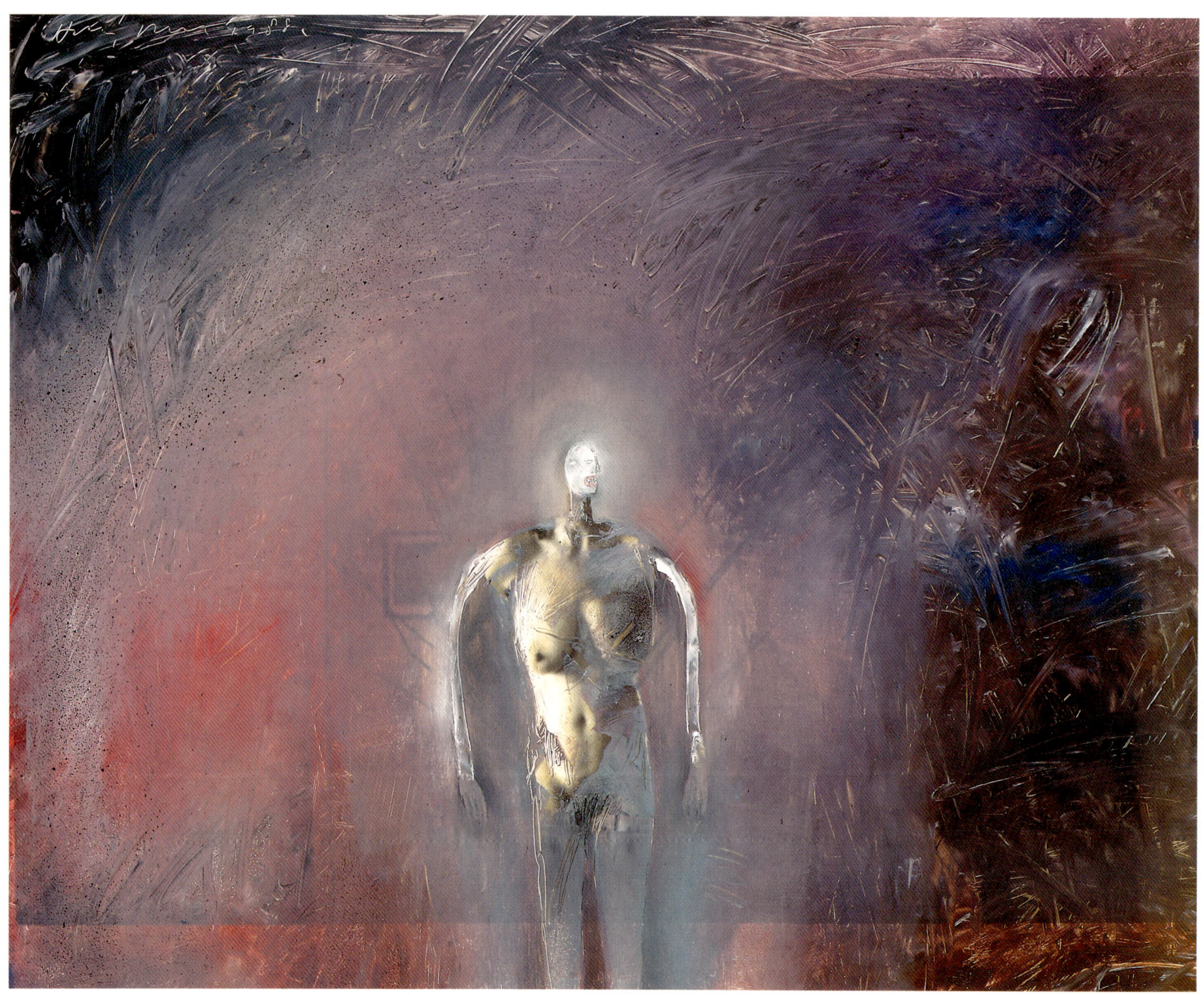

Woman Being Angry (with no clothes), 1986

Oil on silver print; 25" x 30"

Courtesy of Gideon Gartner

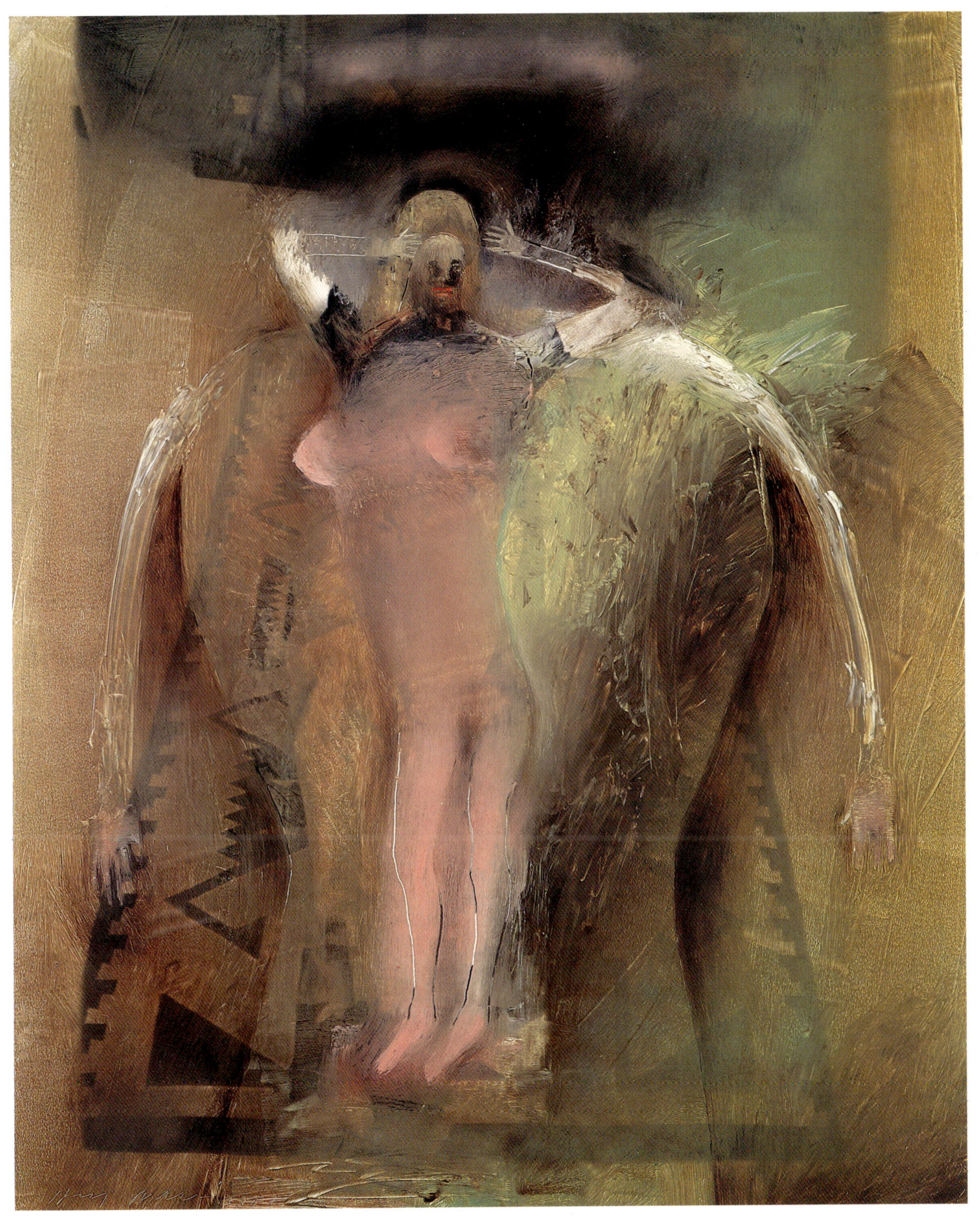

PLATE 20

Woman Dancing Inside Her Mother, 1987

Oil on silver print; 22½" x 18¼"

Courtesy of the artist

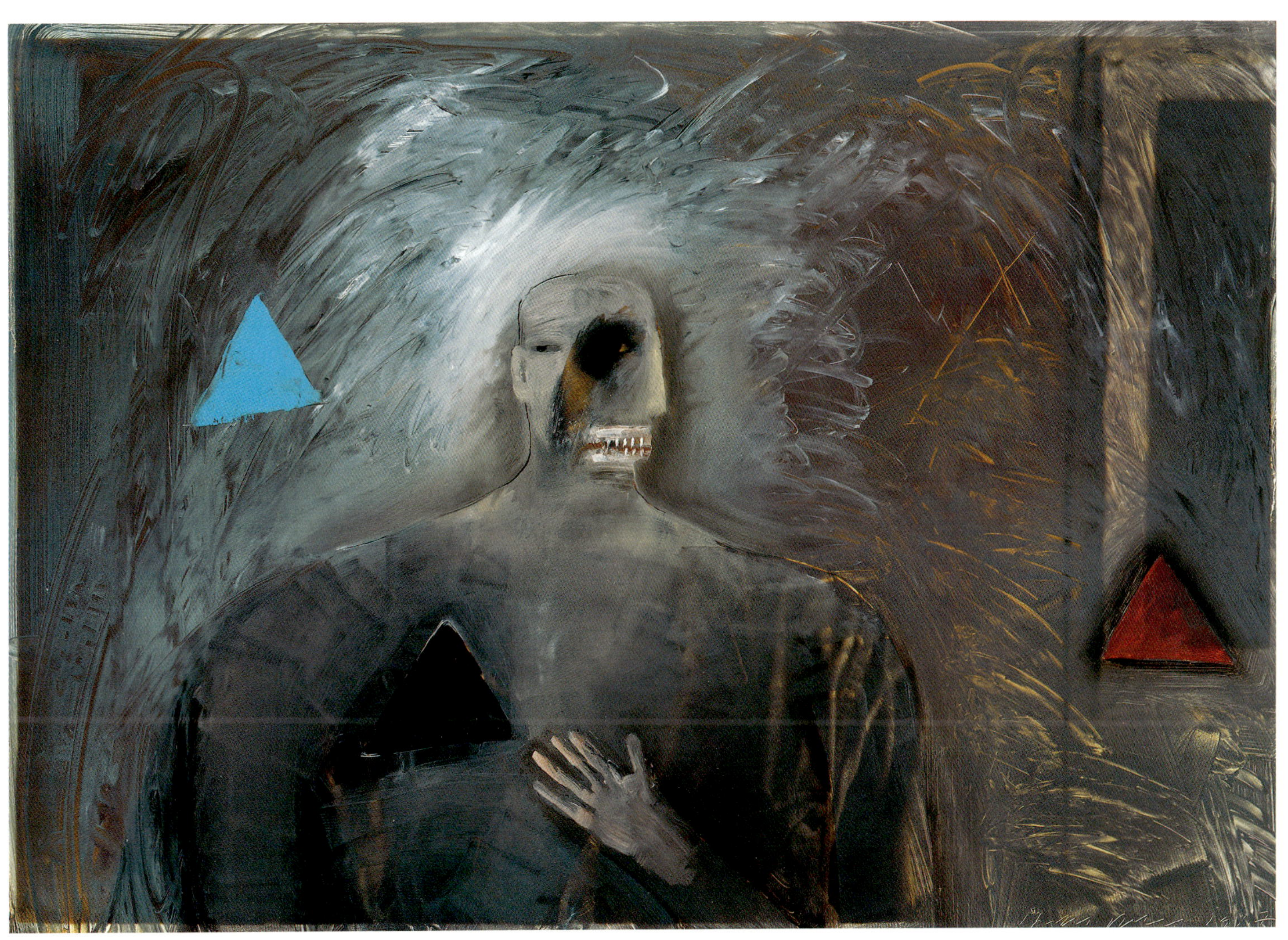

PLATE 21

Man with Triangles, 1987

Oil on silverprint; 23" x 33"

David and Sarajean Ruttenberg

Courtesy of the Ruttenberg Arts Foundation

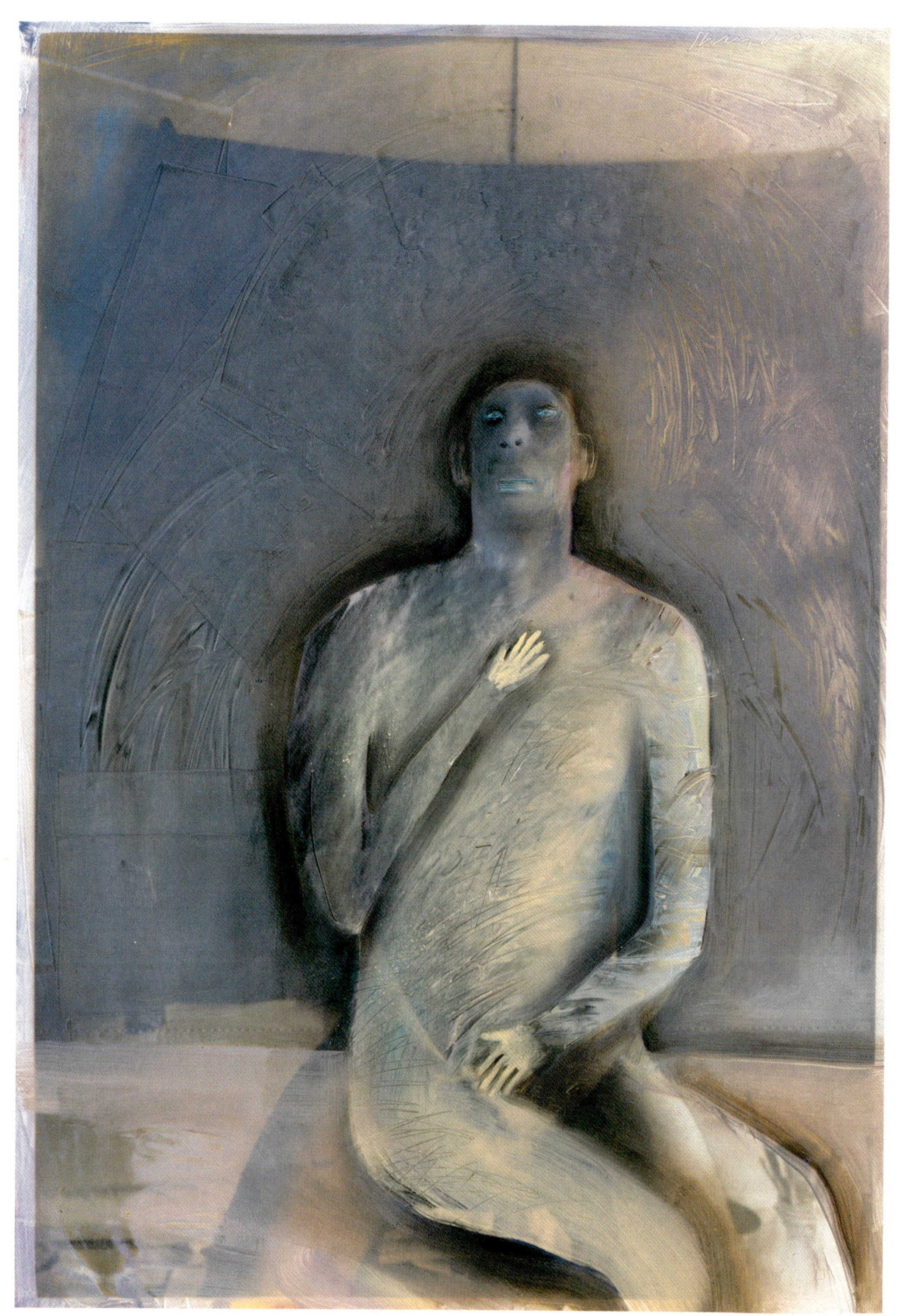

PLATE 22

Man Being Modest, 1987

Oil on silver print; 35" x 25"

Private collection

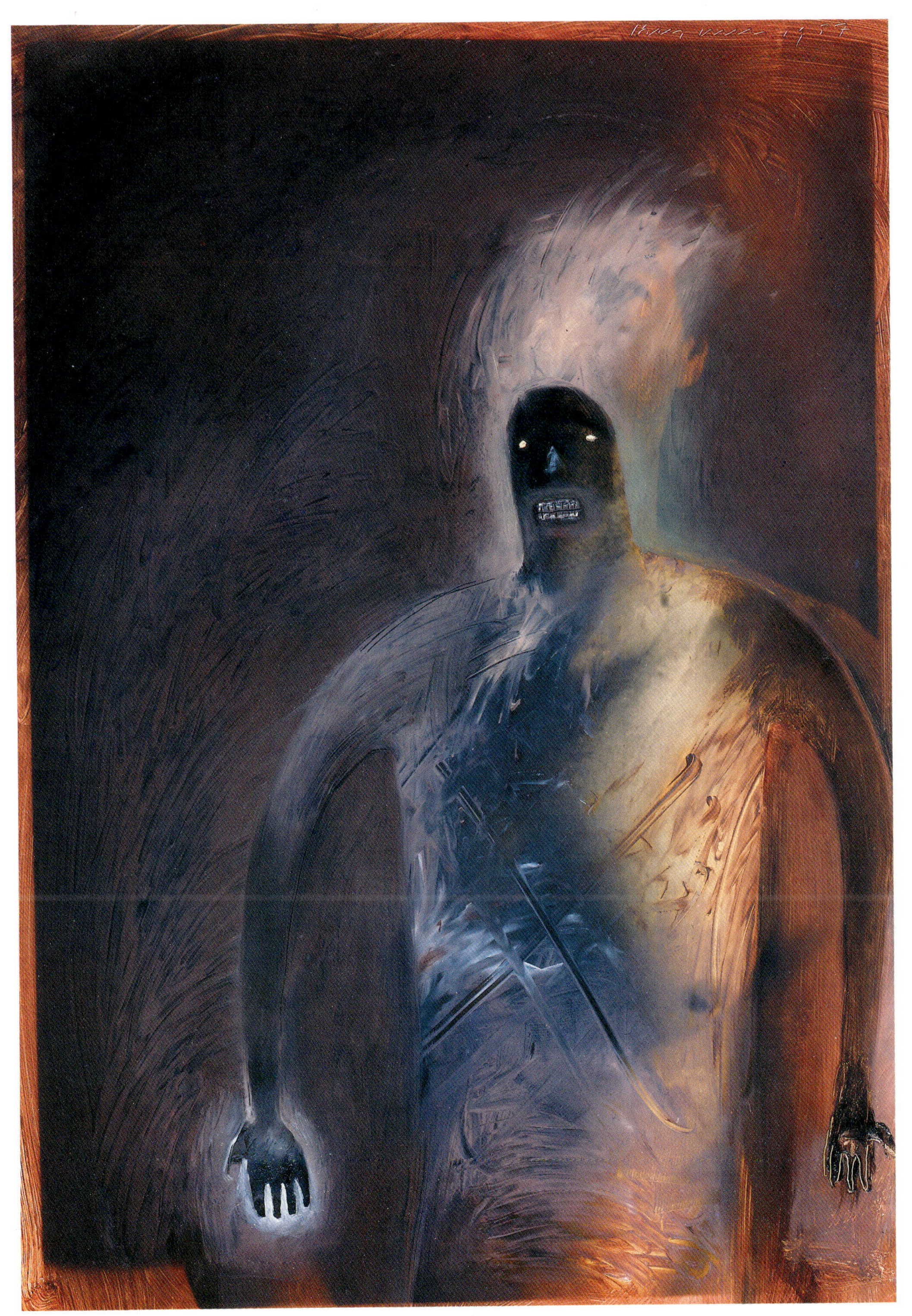

PLATE 23
Boogie Man, 1987

Oil on silver print; 33½" x 23½"
Courtesy of the Graham Nash Collection

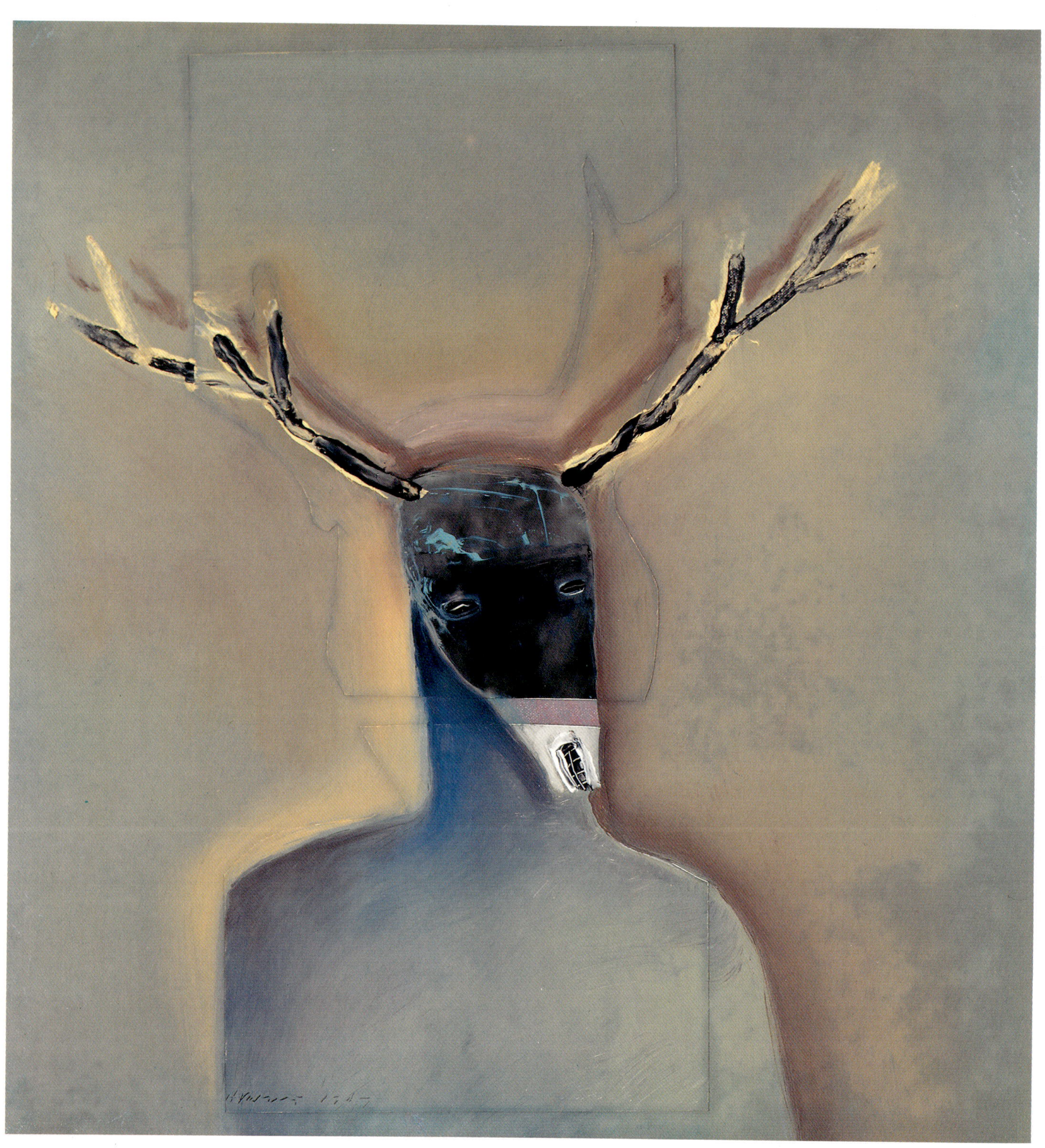

PLATE 24

Deer with Teeth, 1987

Oil on silver print on canvas; 20" x 19"

Courtesy of Alice Killackey

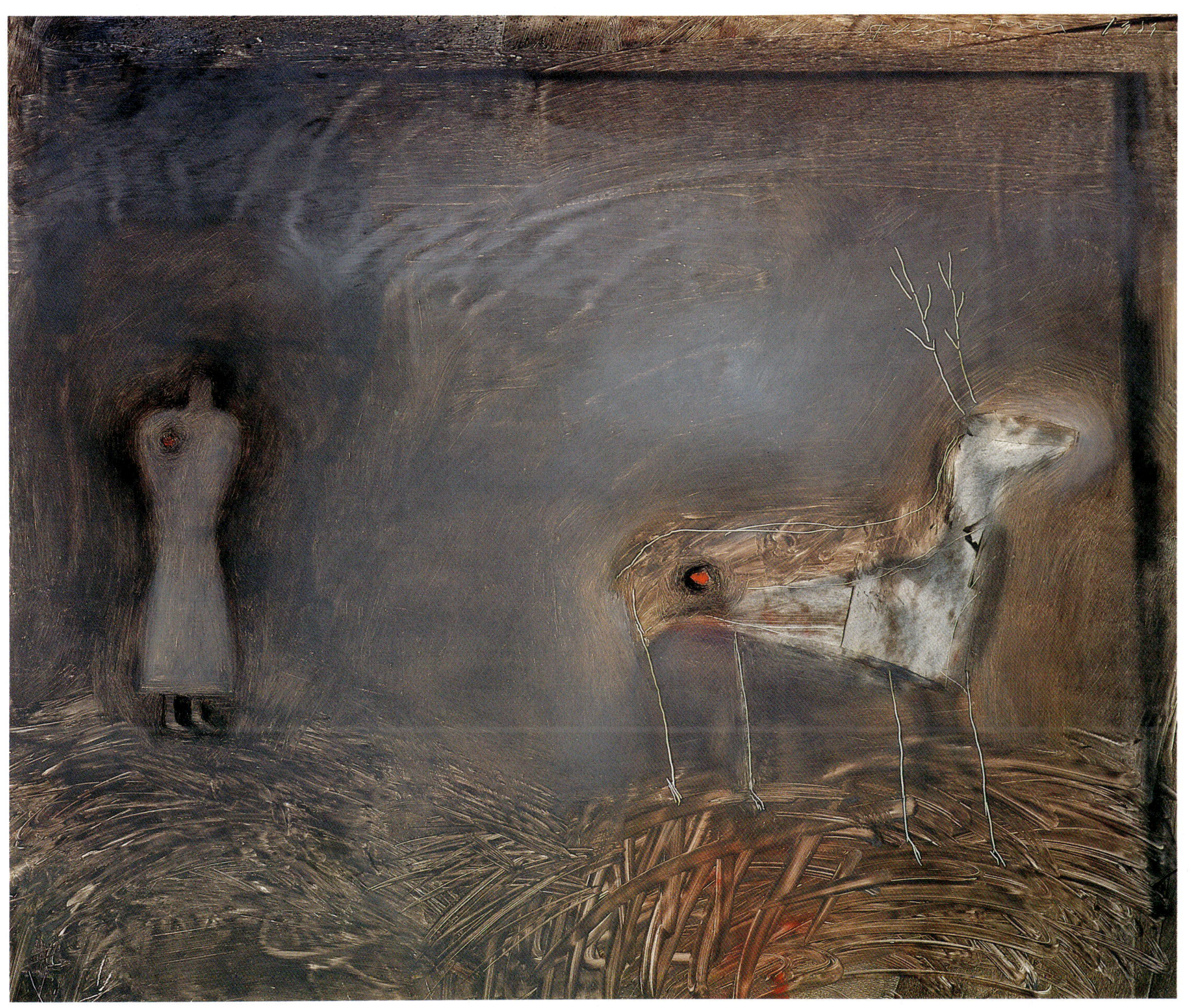

PLATE 25
Deer with Angel, 1987
Oil on silver print; 20" x 24"
Courtesy of the artist

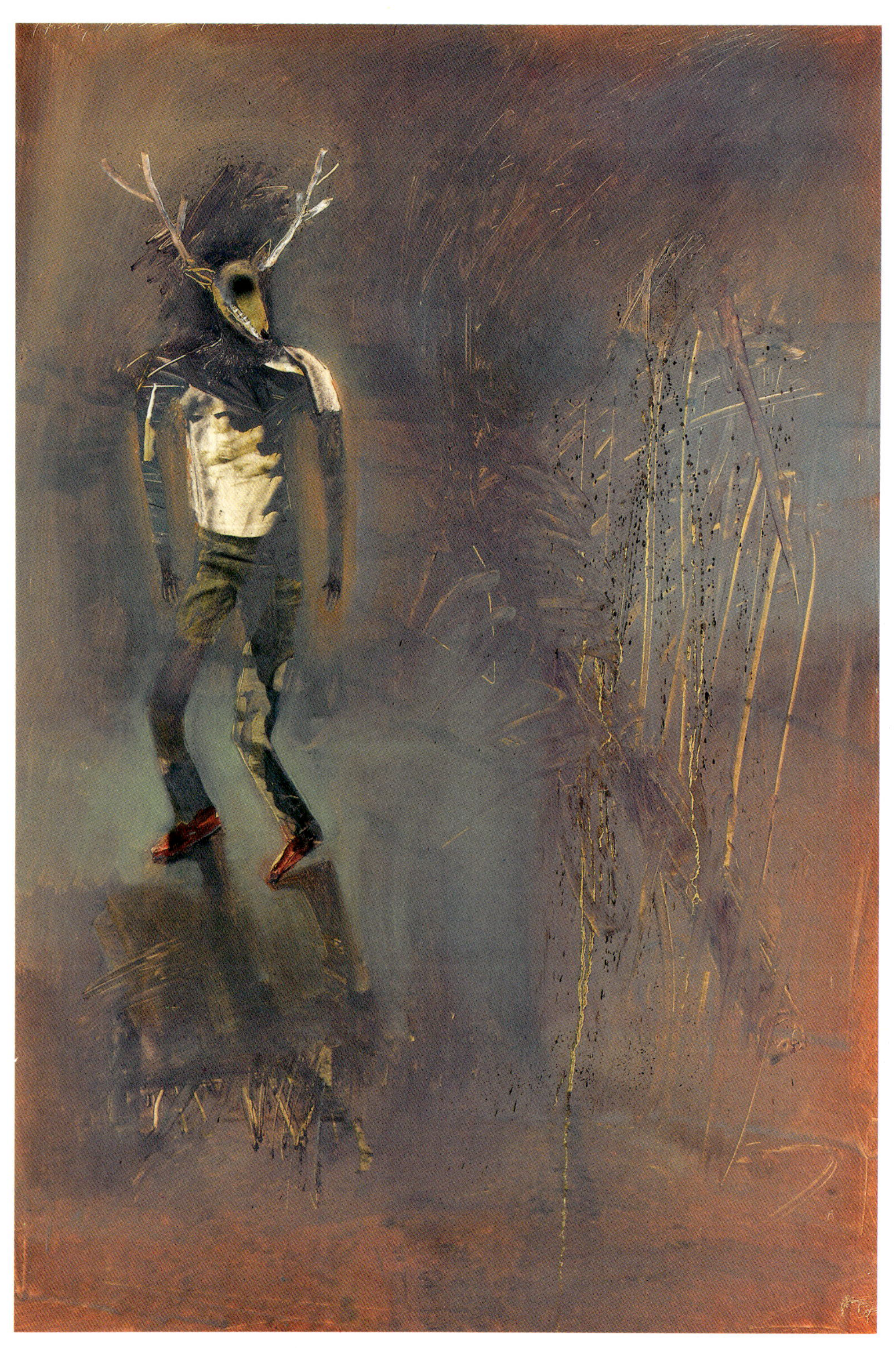

PLATE 26
Boy with Deer Mask, 1987
Oil on silver print; 37½" x 25"
Courtesy of Howard and Bobbie Aidem

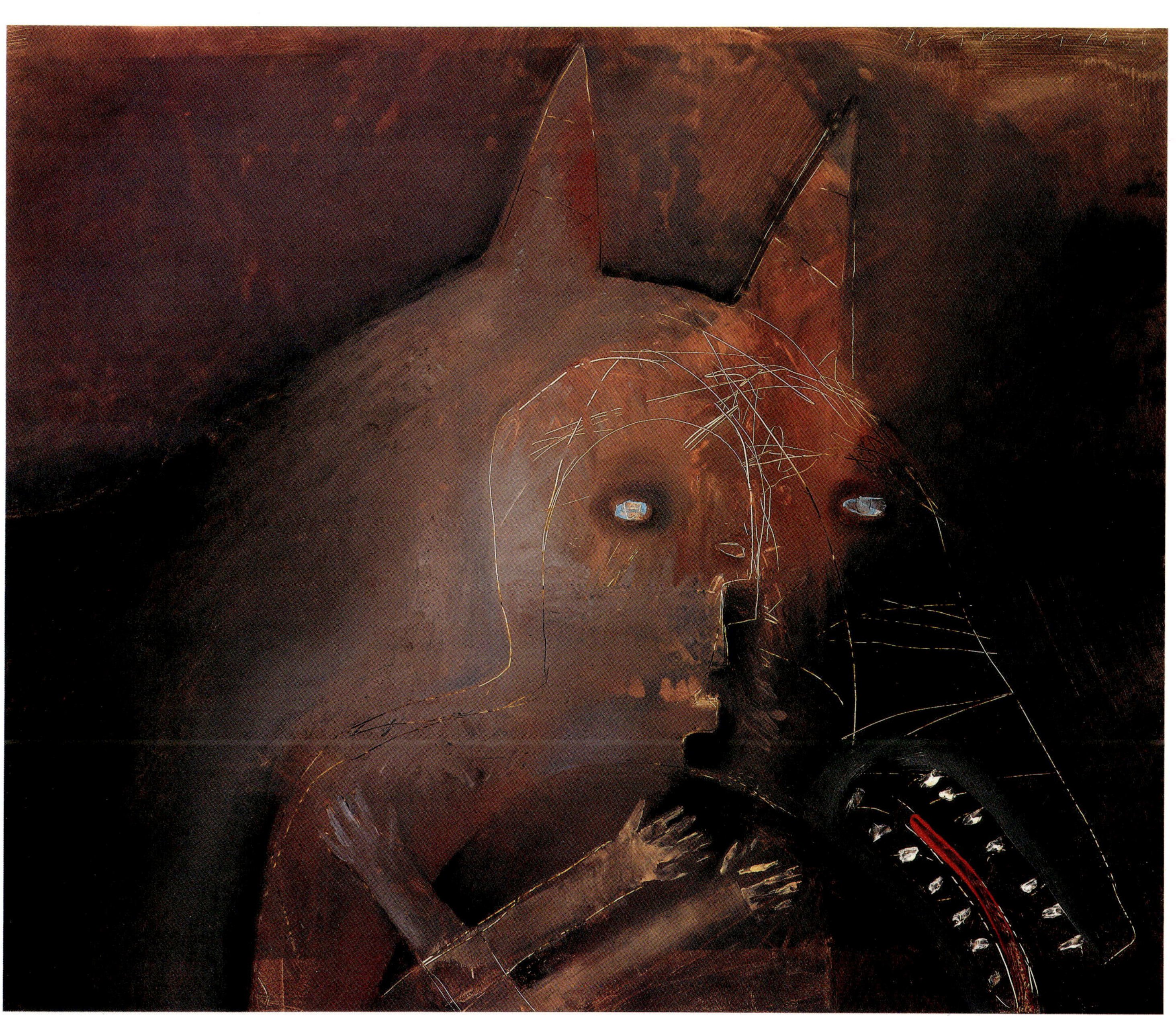

Dog with Man's Head, 1988

Oil on silver print; 25" x 30"

Courtesy of Jane London Salomon

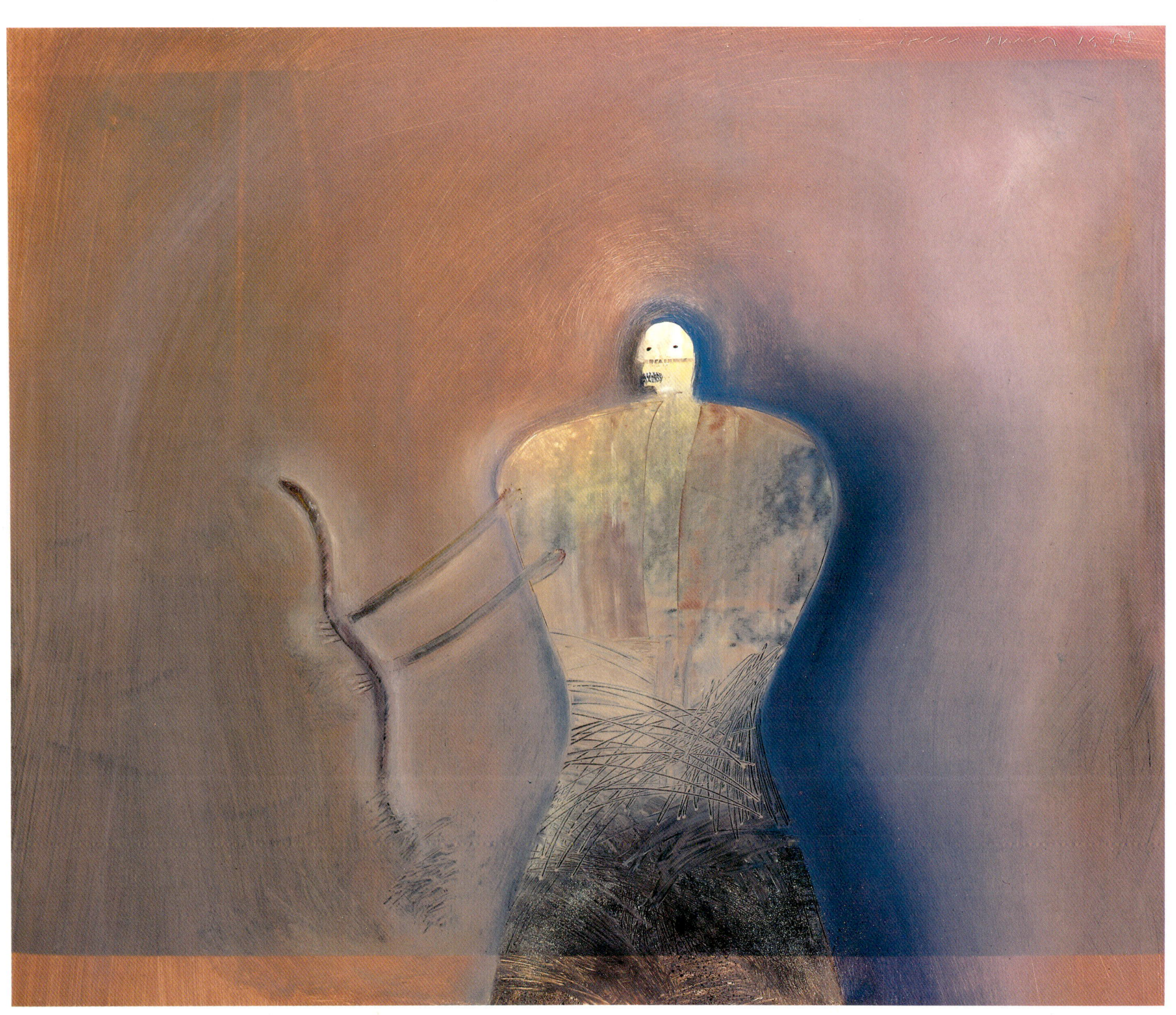

PLATE 28
Snake Handler, 1988
Oil on silver print; 23½" x 28¼"
Courtesy of the artist

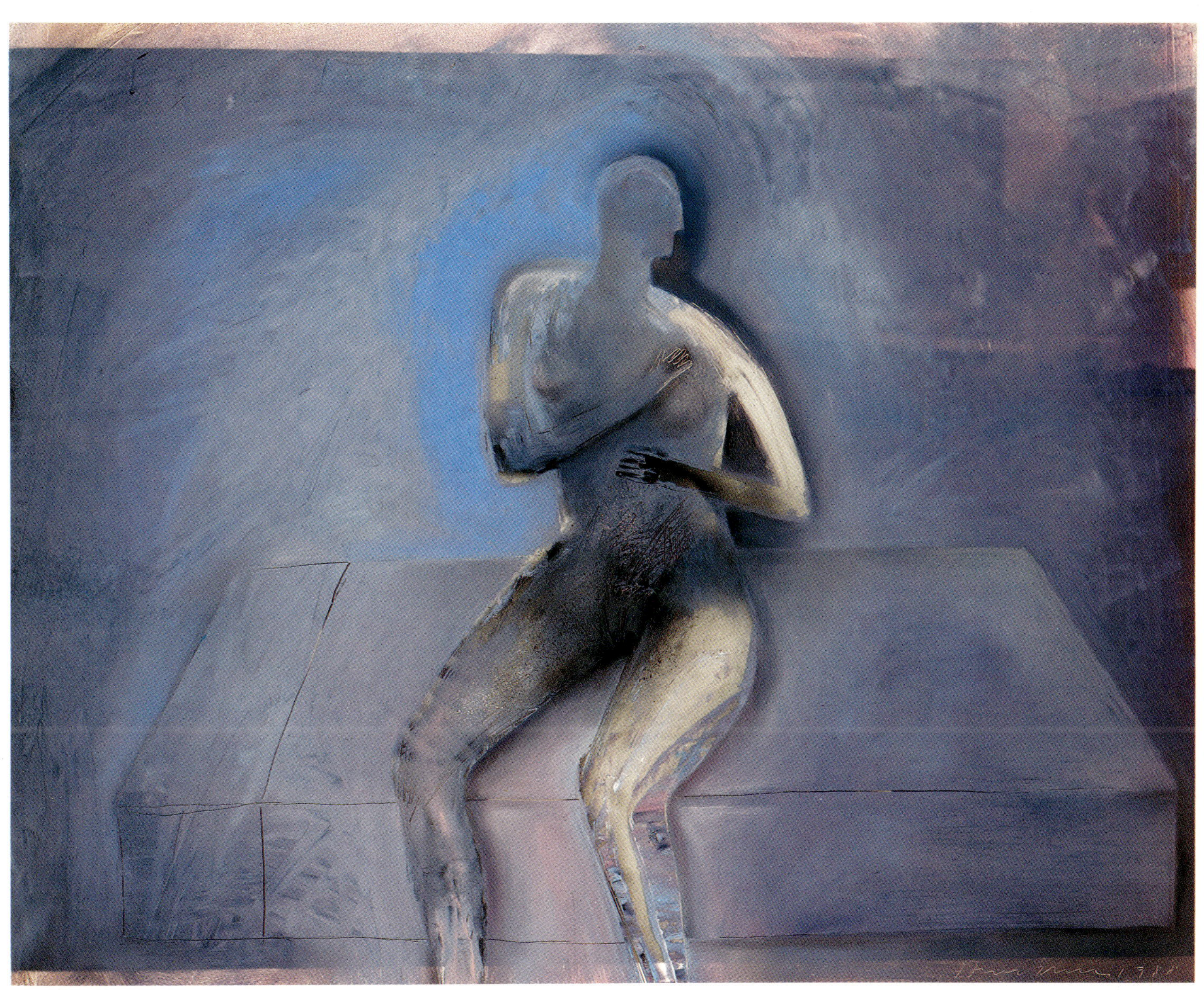

PLATE 29
Woman Sitting Up in Bed, 1988

Oil on silver print; 22½" x 28¾"
Courtesy of Linda Durham

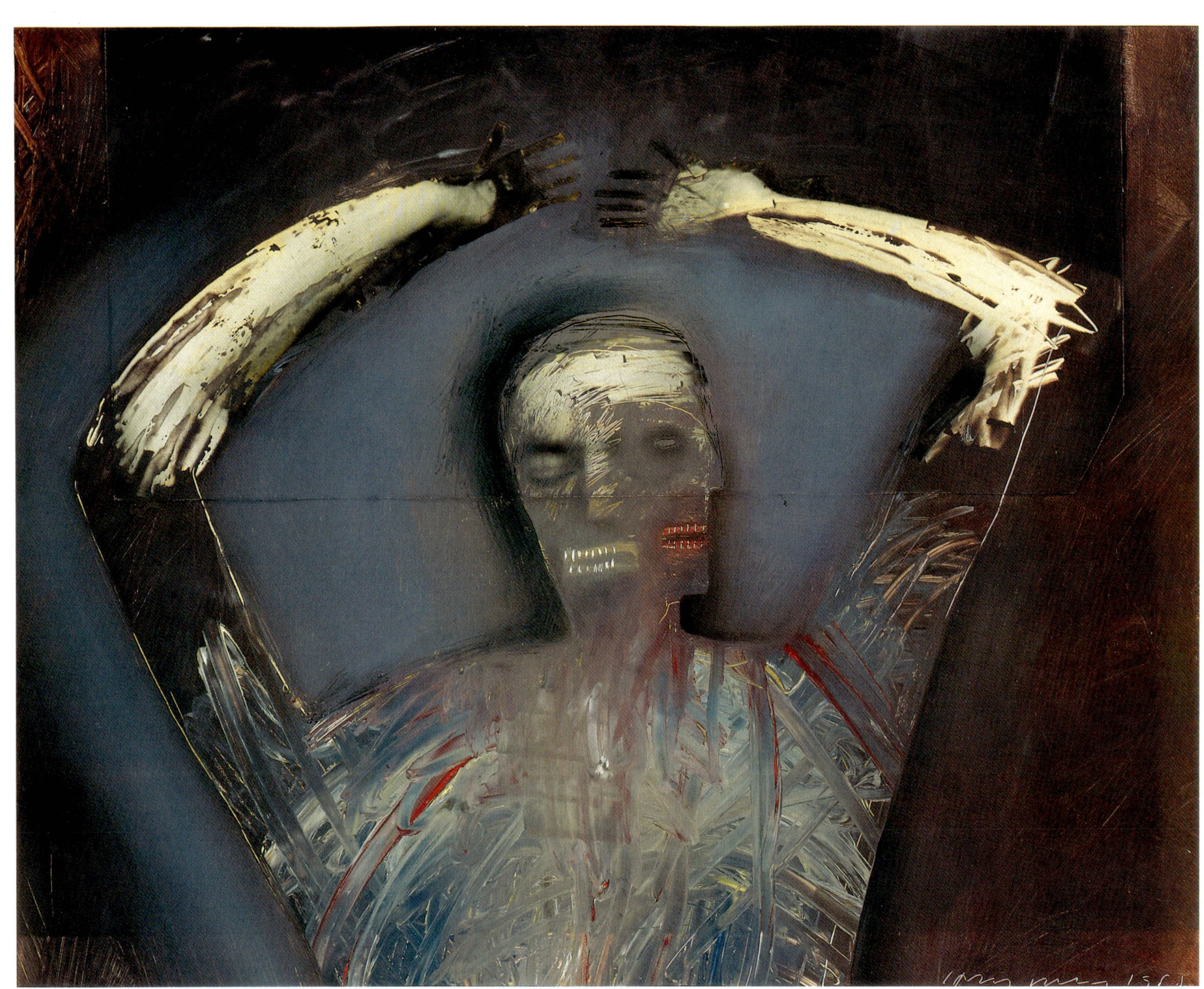

PLATE 30

Man Sleeping (with Arms Raised), 1988

Oil on silver print on canvas; 25" x 30"

Courtesy of Sandy Wade

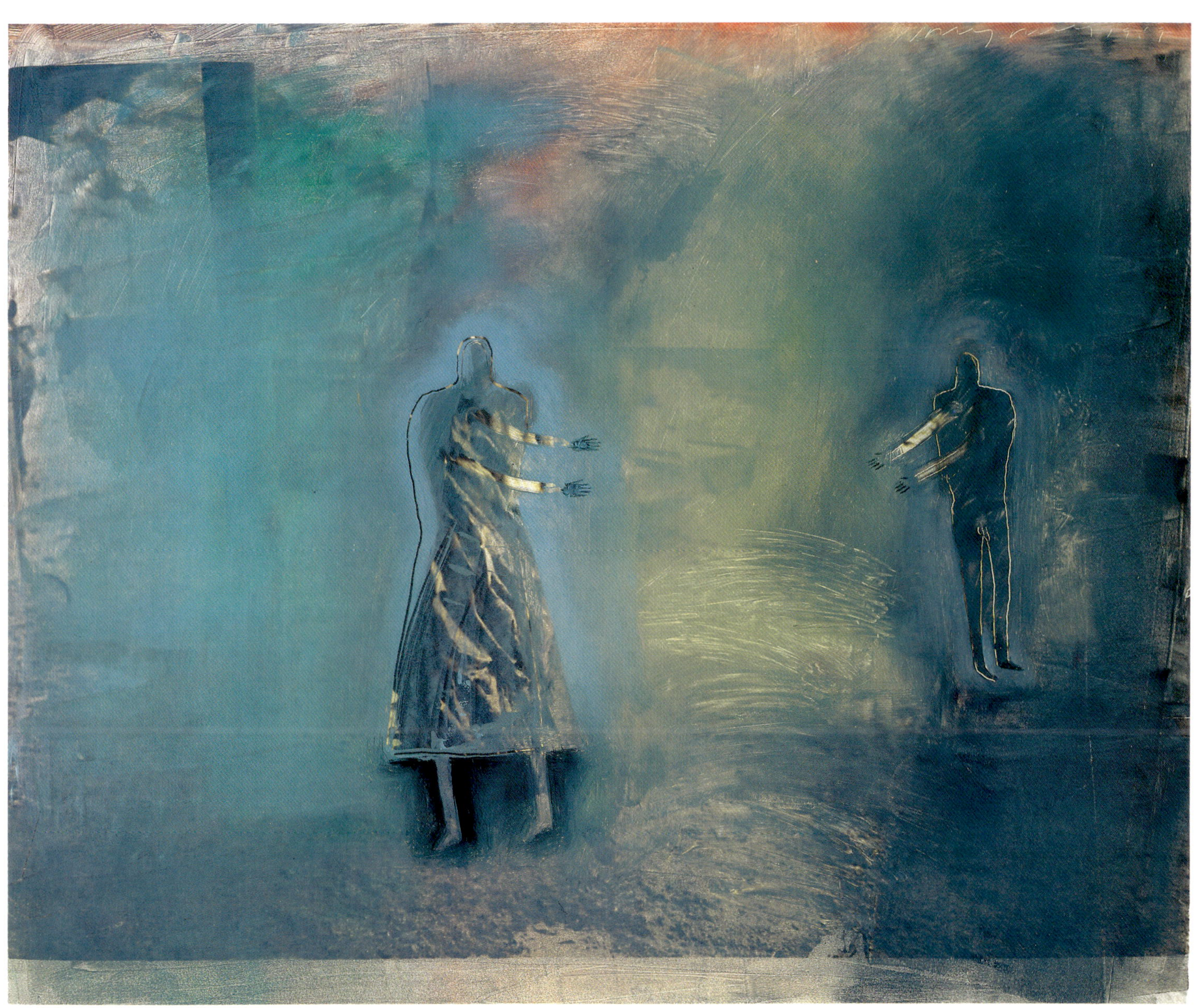

PLATE 31
Couple with Straw, 1988

Oil on silver print; 30" x 25"
Courtesy of the artist

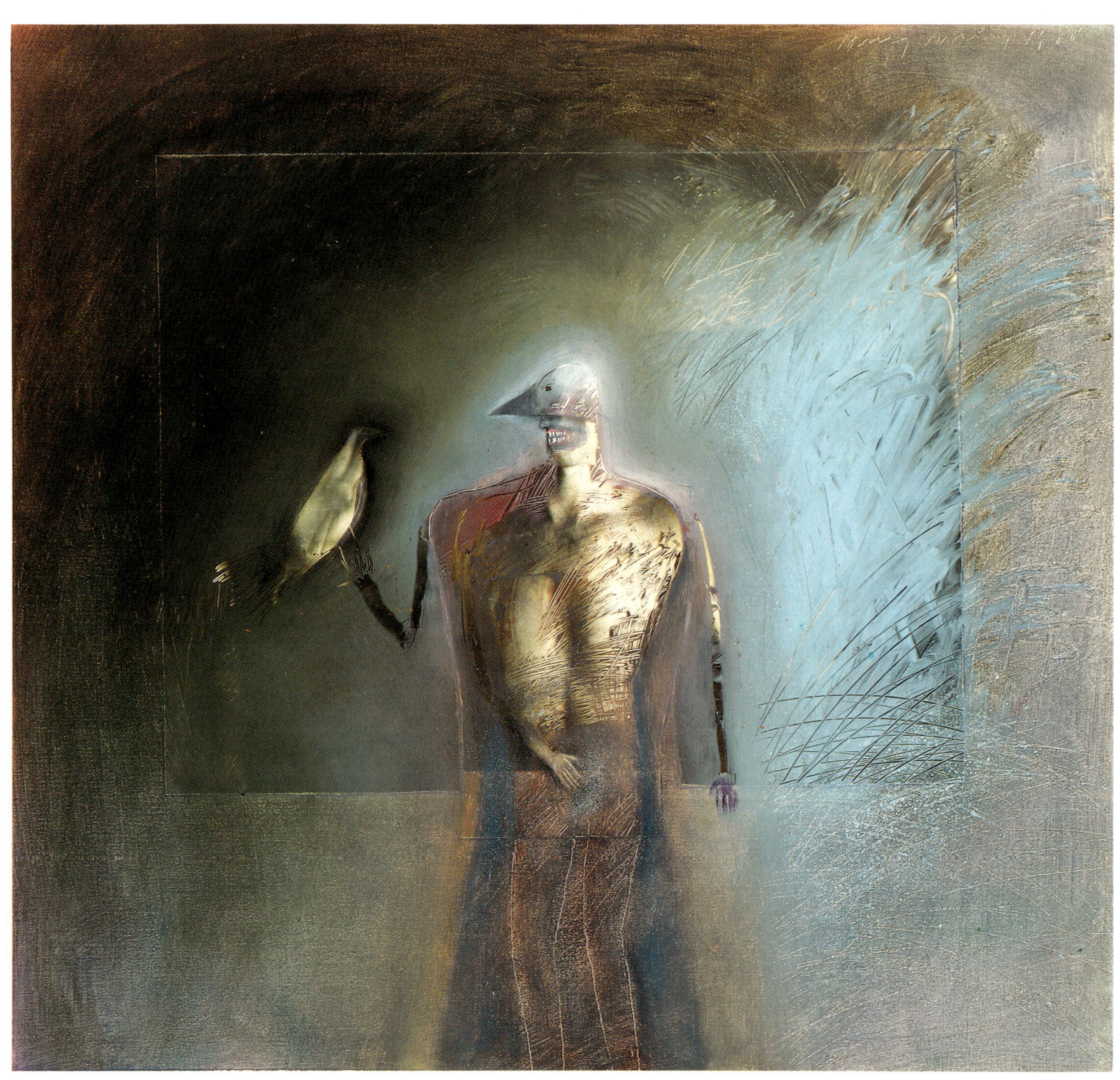

PLATE 32

Man with Two Birds, 1988

Oil on silver print on canvas; 25" x 30"
Courtesy of Kay and Mark Sheridan

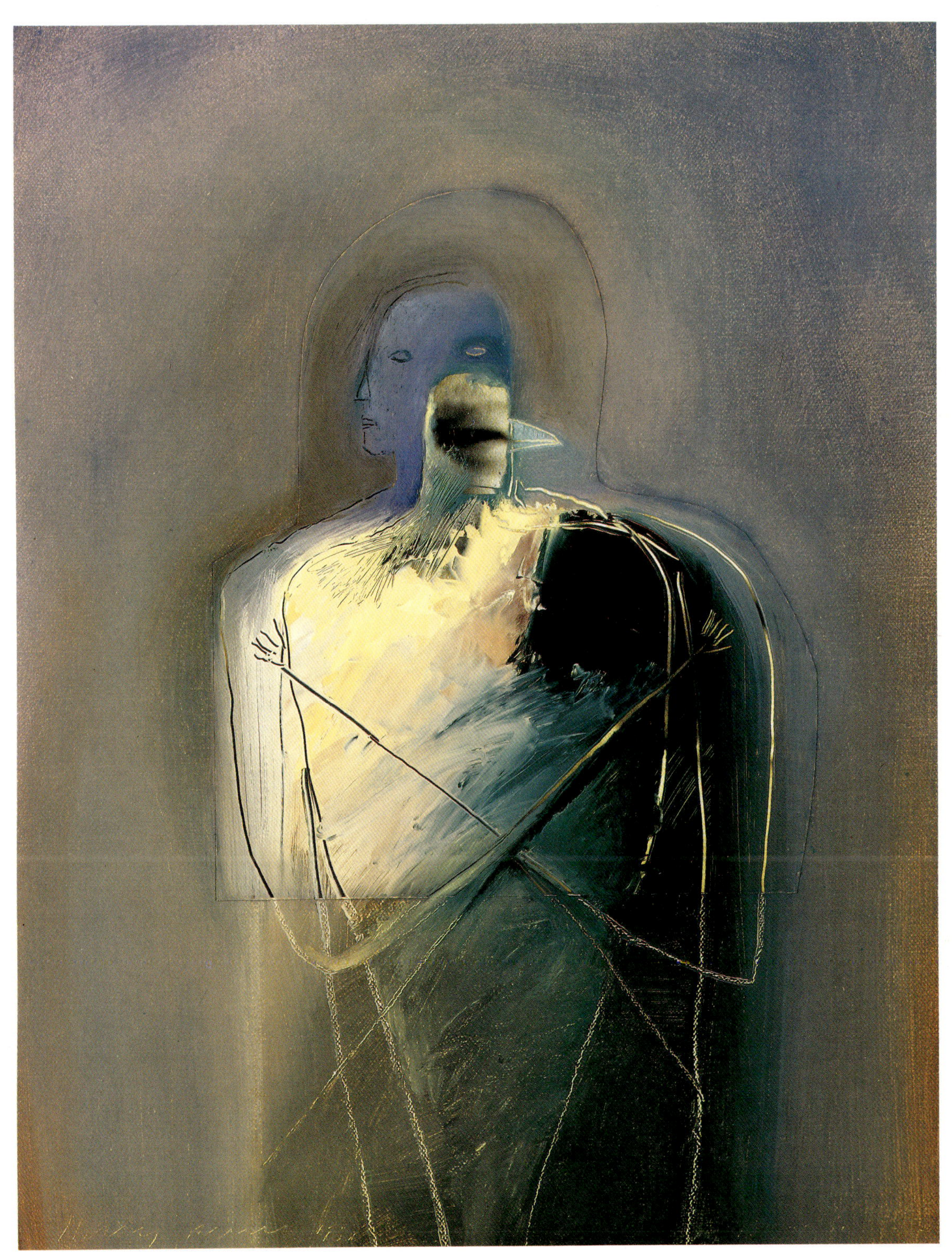

PLATE 33
Bird Being Held, 1989
Oil on silver print on canvas; 15" x 22"
Courtesy of a private collection

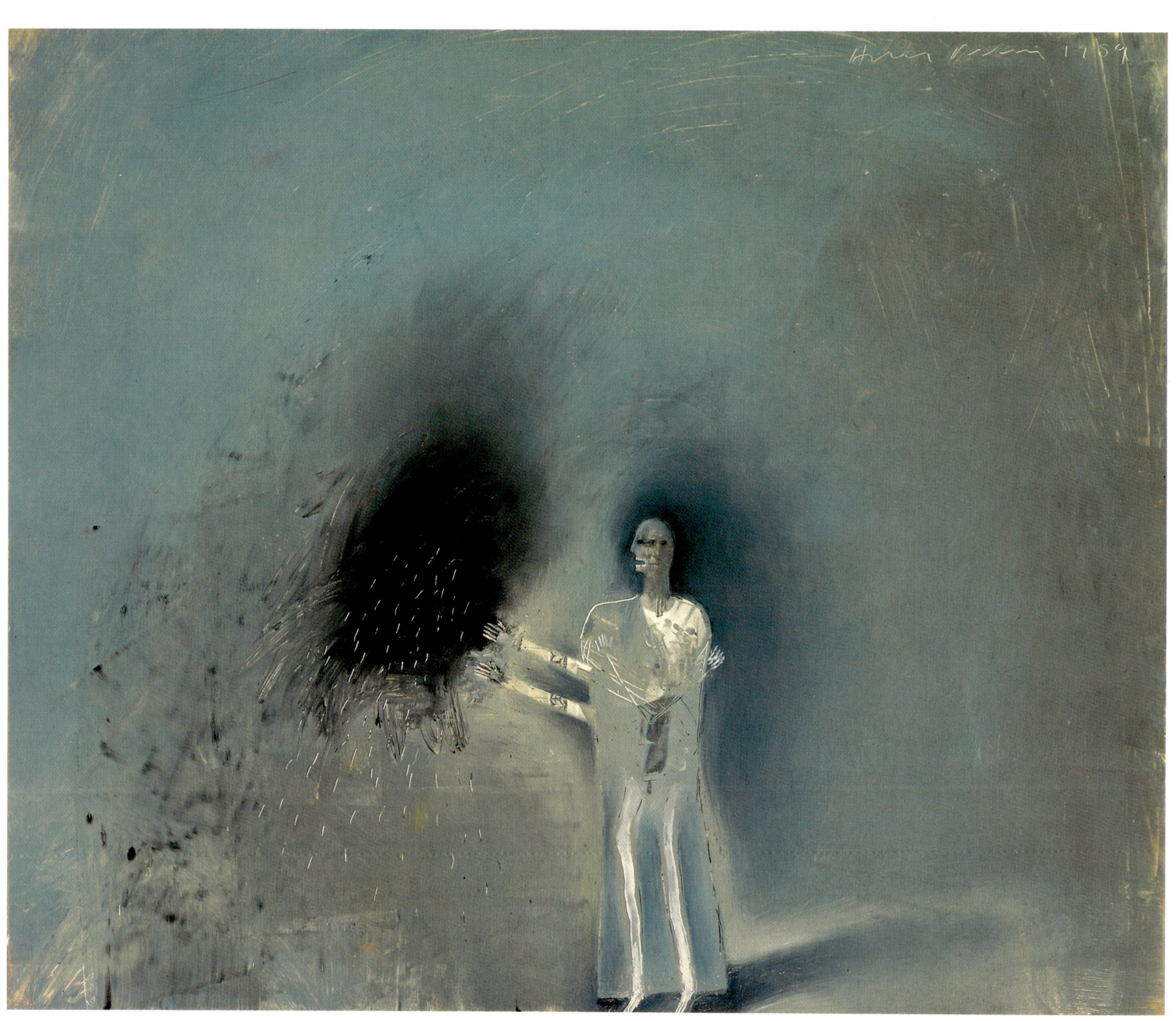

PLATE 34

Woman with Black Cloud, 1989

Oil on silver print; 25" x 30"

Courtesy of the artist

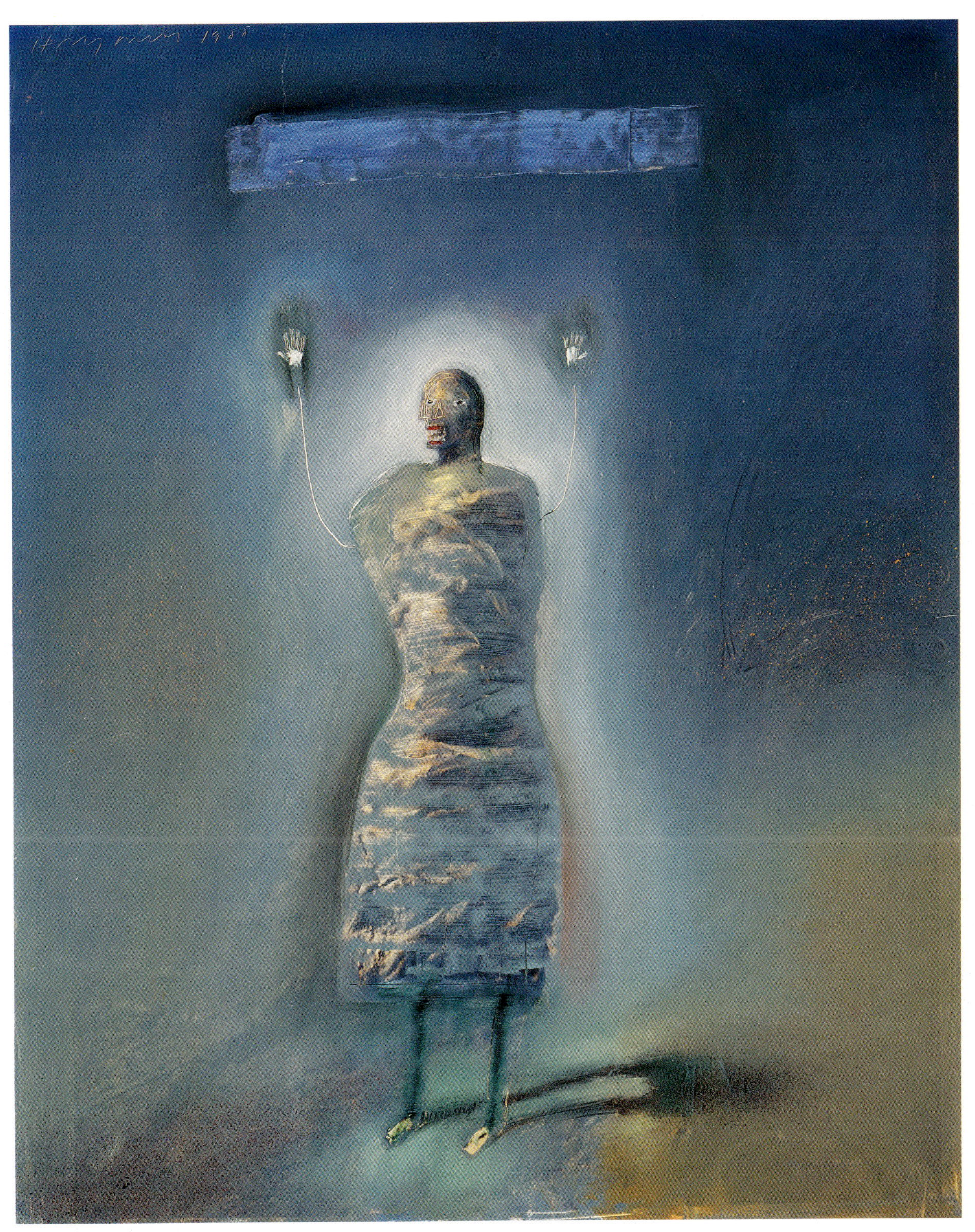

PLATE 35
Woman Being Angry, 1989
Oil on silver print; 28¾" x 23¼"
Courtesy of the artist

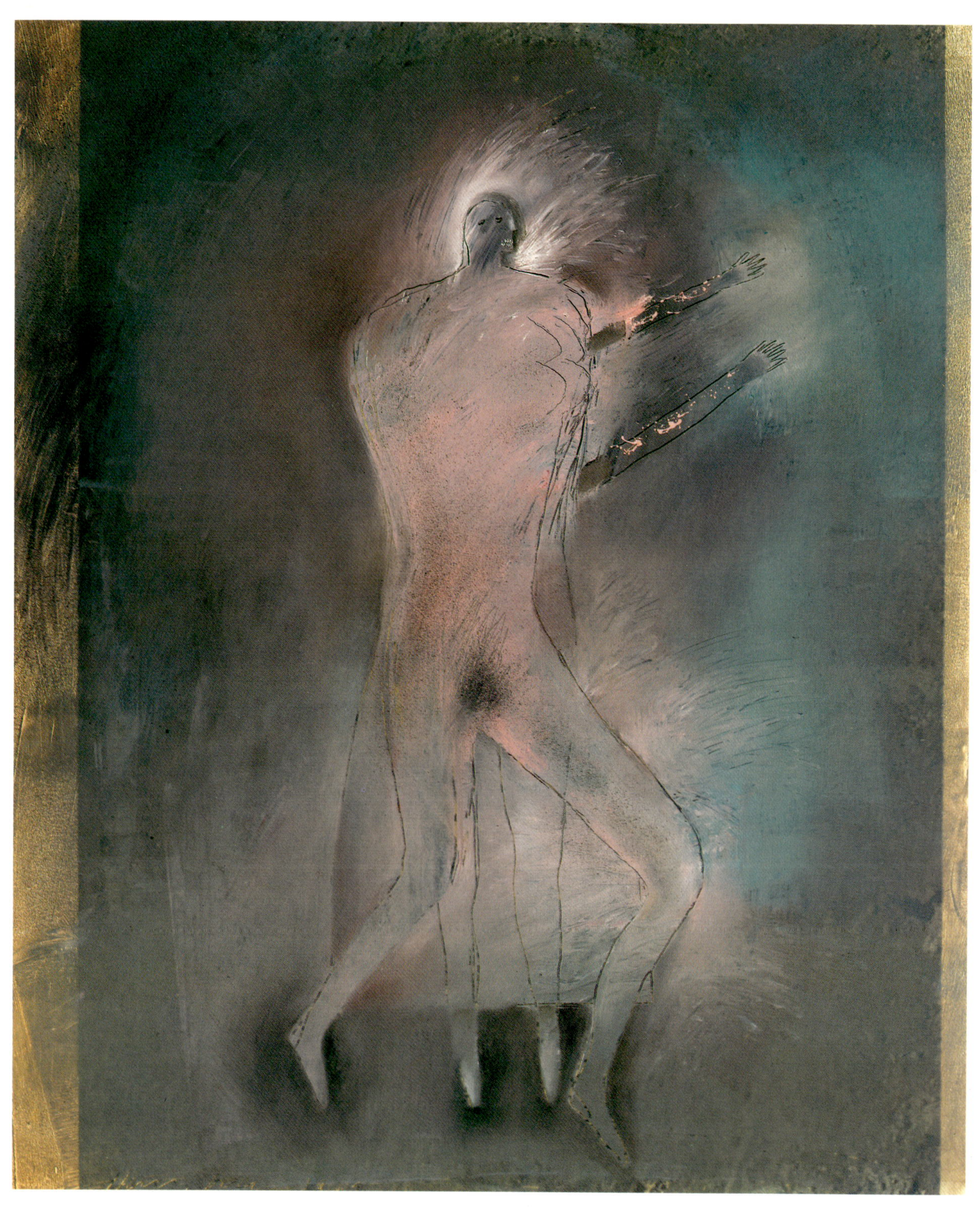

PLATE 36

Woman on Fire, 1989

Oil on silver print; 25" x 30"

Courtesy of the artist

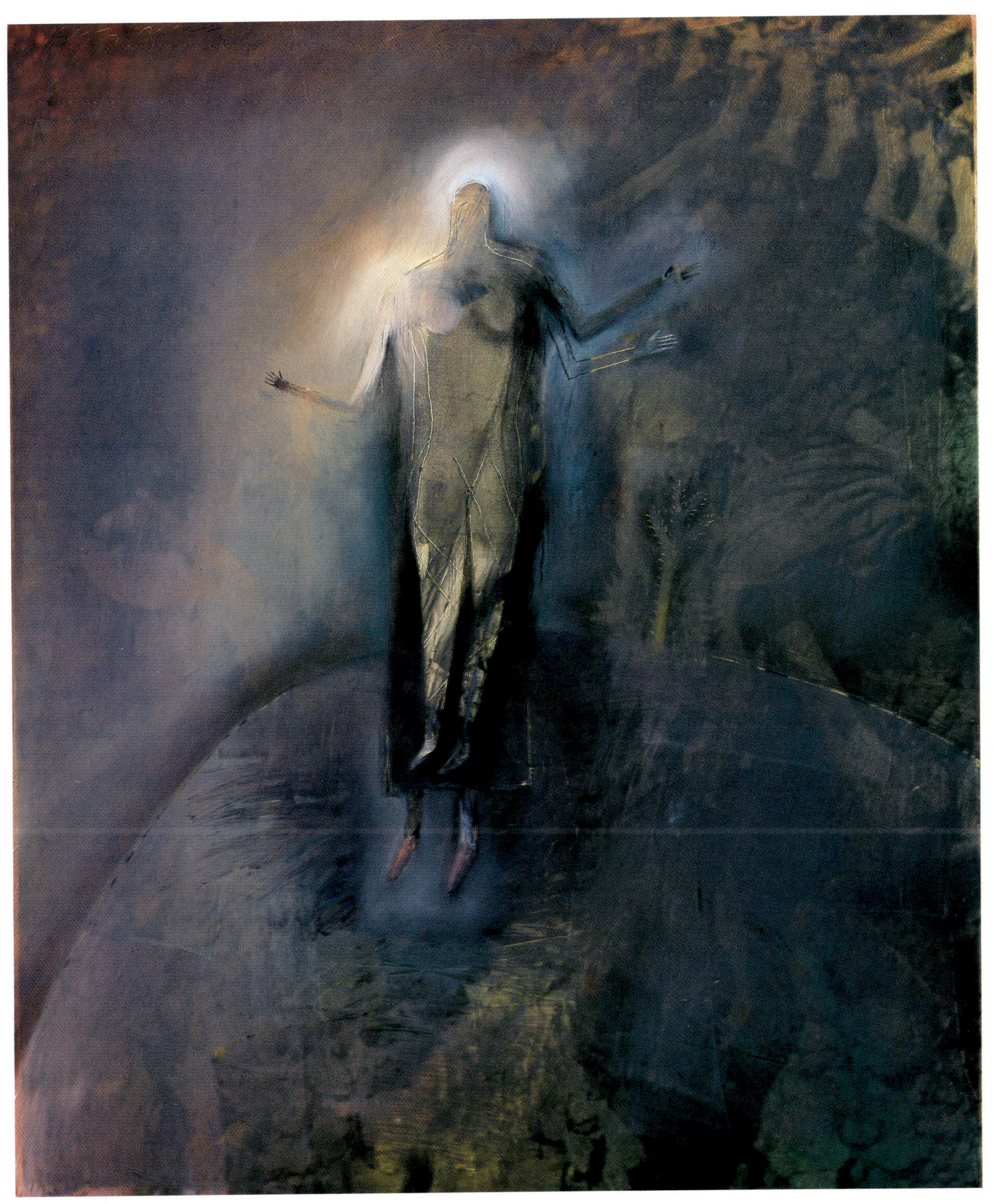

PLATE 37
Woman Dancing on Top of a Hill, 1989
Oil on silver print; 30" x 25"
Courtesy of Dr. and Mrs. Jorge Schneider

Printed and bound in Korea
through Overseas Printing Corporation,
San Francisco, California